from Roger
February 2... ...aiting
for chatolte & Kelise to be born.

11/22

Flavours of Asia

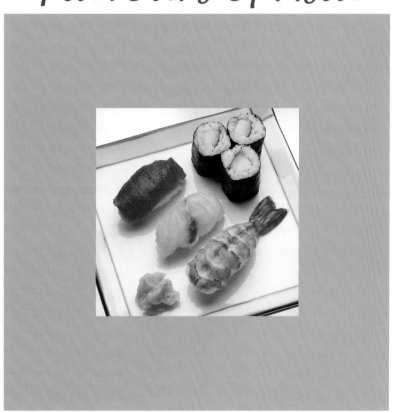

FLAVOURS OF ASIA

Published by
Arden Imprints,
P.O. Box 113, Farnham,
Surrey GU10 5YZ, UK.

ISBN 1 901268 00 4

Photographs on pages 66, 76 and 153 were originated for
The Best of Philippine Cooking by Glenda Barretto
(published by Via Mare, Manila; ISBN 971 91882 0 0)
and are reproduced courtesy of the publisher

Book design: HC Designs, Hong Kong
Jacket design: Centurion Press Group Ltd., London
Colour origination: Elements (UK) Ltd., Leeds

Printed in Hong Kong

Flavours of *Asia*

Edited by
John Mitchell

ARDEN IMPRINTS

Contents

Editor's Notes

Over a period of thirty years I had the good fortune to live in Asia and travel extensively researching, editing and publishing cookbooks and restaurant guides. During that time I accumulated files of more than two thousand recipes, most of which were obtained from the professionals I met ranging from the immaculately-attired, imperious executive chefs overseeing the kitchens of the region's premier hotels to street hawkers, dressed in shorts, t-shirts and flip-flops, perspiring behind their simple roadside food stalls cooking their one-dish speciality.

Having to choose from those files the one hundred and seventy recipes that follow has been extremely difficult and has meant omitting, among others, some of my personal favourites. However, I feel the selection, offering as it does both traditional and less familiar dishes, is representative of the continent's diverse cooking styles.

While personally making no claims to any great culinary skills I have, nonetheless, over the years made some changes to the original recipes which, considering their source, may appear somewhat presumptuous. But, in many cases I felt this was necessary to adapt the offerings of professional, Asian-based chefs for practical use in the average domestic kitchen.

Also, in the case of the earlier books, there was, for many with no easy access to an Asian market, the difficulty of obtaining many of the less familiar and exotic ingredients. Fortunately, however, this is no longer such a factor as nowadays many supermarkets provide shelves dedicated to Asian produce and it is only in the more remote regions of Europe and North America that any difficulties should be encountered. Even so, I would suggest that a visit to your nearest 'Chinatown', or other predominately ethnic district, will prove rewarding and provide even more inspiration to add to your culinary repertoire.

Much of the joy of Asian food, in both cooking and eating, lies in continually trying something new and my early visits to Malaysia and Thailand watching cooks wielding the lids of tobacco tins and other such makeshift 'measuring spoons' to add their own subtle touches to traditional dishes made me appreciate that even those of us who attain no higher status in the gastronomic world than that of enthusiastic amateur should always be prepared to experiment and improvise.

Naturally, the basics must be applied; a *satay sauce* requires peanuts and a *sweet and sour* must be just that. And there would be little point in planning to prepare an Indian curry without a well stocked spice rack to hand or a Thai dinner without lemon grass, basil and a plentiful supply of those little green chillies which local cooks use with such abandon but which have often been known to bring tears to the eyes of many an unwary foreigner.

But that apart, recipes (regardless of their source) should not in my view be strictly adhered to and, in particular, spices should always be measured and blended to suit individual tastes.

A widely held view is that nearly all of the region's food must be essentially 'hot and spicy' but this is not so. Indeed, the classical Chinese cuisine from the southern province of Kwandung, arguably the most universally popular Asian food, and one which has had a considerable influence throughout the whole of South East Asia, is renowned for its mildness and delicate fragrance.

There is, of course, no denying that to retain the authenticity of some dishes (notably those from Thailand, southern India and the western Chinese province of Szechuan) only so much can be done to 'dampen the fire' and these should initially be treated with considerable caution by those with delicate palates and sensitive digestive systems. However, these do tend to be the exceptions.

In reality, the two words which spring to mind to encapsulate the true spirit of Asian cooking are 'balance' and 'harmony'; a balance of spices, herbs, roots and leaves, all carefully blended to enhance the natural flavours of the main ingredient to produce a harmony of taste, aroma, colour and texture designed to appeal to all the senses.

To those unaccustomed to cooking Asian food the process may at first appear to be complicated and time-consuming but, it should be appreciated most of the work lies in the advance preparation (when there is no immediate pressure on feeding hungry mouths) while the cooking itself is usually simple and fast.

A typical home-cooked Asian meal might consist of a soup, three or four main courses (seafood, poultry, meat and vegetable), a selection of condiments, dips and side dishes (soy sauce, chilli sauce, salted eggs and pickles) and the all-important, ubiquitous bowl of rice.

No Chinese meal would be complete without the seemingly bottomless teapot, while in India and Pakistan a cooling glass of lassi (a salted yoghurt drink) makes an ideal liquid refreshment to go with a curry. Although some restaurant menus may offer many tempting desserts, a meal at home is more likely to be concluded with a selection of fresh fruits.

Consistency and style tend to present problems when it comes to editing a cookbook, and this is particularly true when the recipes come from such a variety of sources, as is the case with this book. To misquote the great American, Abraham Lincoln: "You can please some of the cooks all of the time and all of the cooks some of the time but it's nigh on impossible to please all of the cooks all of the time."

There are those who wish each step of each recipe to be explained in great detail, others who find this tedious and an insult to their own initiative. There are those who prefer a clear and simplistic layout with ample white space; others who feel additional recipes would have given better value for money. And, where an indication of '4-6 servings' may seem over generous to some, to others it may well suggest an editor of frugal disposition.

I've tried a number of different approaches but after working on more than forty such books am no nearer to finding the answer. Even referring to the offerings of the best known cookery writers has given little or no guidance as they all have their individual styles, no doubt, in each case, appealing to some while irritating others. I can only hope that the following notes, in effect an explanation of the guide lines set for editing this book, will help you get more enjoyment from using these recipes.

As explained previously I have, over the years, made changes to the recipes and while attempting to remain true to the spirit of the originals have tried to present them in a consistent manner that I hope you will find clear and easy to follow.

However, I've worked on the assumption (fairly I believe) that by choosing to peruse a book of Asian recipes written in English you have expressed a greater than average interest in the culinary arts and will already be familiar with 'kitchen basics', learned at home or school, through the many books on the subject or perhaps, as in my case, through trial and error brought on by the realisation that a home-cooked meal is far more enjoyable than opening a tin, heating-up a ready-cooked meal in the microwave or phoning for a home-delivery pizza.

With this in mind I've chosen in most cases to use the all-embracing term 'clean and prepare' rather than bothering with details such as skinning, scaling, plucking, peeling or scraping.

As Asian family meals are most likely to consist of a number of dishes being served simultaneously, I have not suggested a specific number of servings for each recipe. Rather, the indicated quantities have in mind a meal for four to six people. If a typical Western meal of one, two or three courses is planned you may need to make appropriate adjustments.

Nevertheless, in planning the layout of the book I decided to include a section headed 'Snacks and Starters'. This seemed to be a happy compromise for while Asians don't regularly have a separate starter they certainly do eat snacks at all times of the day and night. And most seem able to do so without showing a steady increase in girth which is a mystery (and, indeed, mildly irritating) to those of us with less fortuitous metabolisms.

To the best of my knowledge, the wok, that most versatile of kitchen utensils, is a Chinese invention and so I have used the name throughout the book although similar pans may go under a different name in other countries, for example the Thais use a krate while in India it is referred to as a kori.

While there are many ways to 'spice-up' a recipe the most flexible way to adjust the 'bite' is with the quantity and choice of chillies, which can range from mild to hot to very hot to "whoaaa".

The general rule is that the smaller they are the hotter they are but be prepared for the occasional 'big red' that proves the exception to the rule.

The quantities given in the following recipes where chillies feature are meant to result in moderately hot dishes but this can only be a personal opinion. The final decision must be yours.

One further point. After topping and tailing and removing the hard ribs comes the decision about the seeds. These are the very heart of the chilli and are more than likely to be discarded by all but the most intrepid 'fire-eaters'. I usually let a few fall into the curry pot but ensure there is some yoghurt or coconut milk nearby just in case, come the final tasting, things have got a little out of hand. But do be sure to add some of the seeds to soy sauce and vinegar when you require a spicy side-dip.

There is considerable similarity between the food and cooking styles of many countries, for example between the basic curries of southern India and Sri Lanka, the delicately spiced dishes of Pakistan and the northern Indian states and the many coconut-flavoured curries of Indonesia and Malaysia.

With this in mind, for each recipe I have named the country where I first came across that particular dish although I have quite often done a little 'mixing and matching' as and when similar recipes have come my way.

The Chinese recipes were collected in Beijing, Shanghai, Hong Kong, Singapore and Taiwan and, while many of those dishes are universally popular, I have, once again, indicated my original source.

As Hong Kong was my home for more than twenty years and was where I was introduced to the multi-delights of Chinese cuisine, I have noted the recipes obtained there apart from the rest of China. This, in spite of the fact that since 1997 Hong Kong has proudly flown the Chinese flag.

The recipe titles are given using a phonetic spelling and so will vary from region to region. The English sub titles are intended as descriptive and not precise translations.

Although China is increasing its production of grape wines, the traditional wine is still distilled from rice. As with most things, quality and cost can vary considerable. The finest wine is said to come from Shaoxing in Eastern China and I can confirm that a glass (or two) of this soft yellow liquid adds to the enjoyment of the meal. However, it is really too good for any but the most exotic cooking pot and a medium priced rice wine is quite adequate for the kitchen cupboard. A medium-dry sherry is often suggested as a substitute but, considering the small cash outlay involved, I would suggest you get the real thing.

Although there is a glossary towards the end of the book, I thought it worth mentioning one particular ingredient at the beginning as it appears frequently in the recipes and there really is no substitute.

Shrimp paste has absolutely nothing in common with the popular sandwich spread sold in little jars.
The dried paste used frequently in South east Asian cooking is black, has a very pungent smell and is sold in cans or small blocks. Crumbled and pounded with other spices it adds a unique and strong flavour and should be used sparingly.

It will keep for long periods but be sure to store in a tightly-sealed container otherwise the odour will invade your kitchen.

It is commonly marketed under its Malaysian name of Blachan. In Indonesia it is called Trasi and in Thailand kapi.

Measurements in this book are based on the metric system, with quantities, under 50 grams (50 g) or 50 millilitres (50 ml) being shown in tablespoons (Tbsp) or teaspoons (tsp). Where ingredients are shown in units without a corresponding size, for example 2 onions or 2 tomatoes, the reference is to medium size.

However, it should be stressed that Asian cooks are less likely to regard precise measurements in such awe as so many of their Western counterparts and, I repeat, where spices are concerned, quantities must always be judged to cater for individual tastes.

And so, while my intention is that the recipes as written will give you pleasure, both in the kitchen and at the table, I sincerely hope, that you will also regard them as the foundations on which to add personal measures of ingenuity and talents and so create your own very special flavours of Asia.

J.M.

Snacks & Starters

TSE MA HAR DOR SI (sesame prawn toast), *recipe page 14*

TSE MA HAR DOR SI (sesame prawn toast)   *Hong Kong*

450 g fresh prawns
1 egg white, lightly beaten
1 tsp minced garlic
1 Tbsp light soy sauce
2 tsp cornflour

0.5 tsp freshly ground black pepper
8 slices white bread
2 Tbsp white sesame seeds
oil for deep frying

Shell and de-vein the prawns and chop very finely. Combine the prawn, egg, garlic, soy sauce, cornflour and pepper to produce a thick, smooth paste.

Remove crusts from the bread and spread a generous layer of the prawn paste on each slice, then sprinkle with sesame seeds.

Heat the oil in a wok until it starts to smoke, then lower heat slightly and deep-fry the prawn slices until crispy and golden.

Remove with a slotted spoon and drain on kitchen paper, then cut into fingers and serve with a side dip of chilli sauce.

TINUKTOK (coconut shrimp parcels)   *Philippines*

450 g fresh shrimps
1 young (green) coconut
1 onion, finely chopped
2 tsp finely chopped ginger
1 tsp finely chopped garlic
2 tsp soft brown sugar

0.5 tsp salt
0.5 tsp freshly ground pepper
1.5 Tbsp fresh lime juice
400 ml thick coconut milk
12 cabbage leaves,
  cut into 12 cm squares

Shell and de-vein the shrimps and chop into small pieces. Cut the coconut in half, discard the water and scoop out the soft flesh. Chop the flesh and place in a bowl together with the shrimps.

Add the onion, ginger, garlic, sugar, salt, pepper, lime juice and 50 ml coconut milk and pound to produce a thick paste.

Lay the cabbage leaves on a flat surface and place on top of each a little of the shrimp mixture. Fold into triangles and secure with toothpicks.

Pour the remaining coconut milk into a wok, bring to the boil and add the stuffed leaves. Cover the pan and cook until most of the liquid becomes thick, then transfer the parcels to a serving platter, open up and spoon a little thick sauce on top.

ZHI MA XIA (sesame prawns)   *Singapore*

12 fresh king prawns
2 tsp finely chopped spring onion
1 tsp finely chopped red chilli
1 tsp shredded ginger
1 tsp minced garlic
100 ml Chinese wine
1 Tbsp light soy sauce
1 tsp sugar
0.5 tsp freshly ground black pepper
egg wash
100 g plain flour
oil for deep frying

Shell and de-vein the prawns, leaving tails intact. With a sharp knife, slit the prawns along the back, three quarters way through, then flatten out in butterfly style and place in a shallow dish.

Mix together the onion, chilli, ginger, garlic, wine, soy sauce, sugar and pepper and pour over the prawns. Set aside for 20 minutes, turning the prawns once.

Dip the prawns in the egg-wash and dust with flour, then dip in sesame seeds.

Heat the oil in a wok until very hot and deep-fry the prawns until golden and crispy. Remove with a slotted spoon and drain on kitchen paper.

XIA WAN (prawn cutlets)   *Singapore*

12 fresh king prawns
salt and freshly ground pepper
2 Tbsp Chinese wine

4 eggs, lightly beaten with
3 Tbsp cornflour
75 g fine breadcrumbs

Shell and de-vein the prawns, leaving tails intact. With a sharp knife, slit the prawns along the back, three-quarters way through, then flatten out in butterfly style. Sprinkle with salt, pepper and wine and set aside for 10 minutes.

Dip the prawns in the beaten egg, then coat with breadcrumbs.

Heat the oil until it starts to smoke, then lower heat slightly and deep-fry the prawns until golden and crispy. Drain off excess oil before serving.

CHAO TOM (puréed shrimp on sugar cane) *Vietnam*

450 g fresh shrimps
1 tsp oyster sauce
75 g pork fat
5 cloves garlic, chopped
3 spring onions, finely chopped
1 tsp brown sugar

2 tsp fish sauce
3 Tbsp cornflour
1 egg-white, lightly beaten
10 12cm pieces sugar cane
* cut in half, lengthways*
ginger sauce

Shell and de-vein the shrimps and rub evenly with oyster sauce. Set aside for 15 minutes then chop finely. Boil the pork fat for 5 minutes, then drain and cut into small pieces.

Place the shrimp, pork, spring onion, garlic, sugar and pepper in a mortar and pound until smooth, then add the fish sauce, cornflour and egg-white. Mix thoroughly., then set aside in the refrigerator for 30 minutes.

Shape the paste around pieces of sugar cane, leaving a small space at each end. Cook under a hot grill, or over charcoal, for 3-5 minutes, turning occasionally, until golden. Serve immediately with a side dish of ginger sauce.

BANH MI CHIEN (prawn toast) *Vietnam*

300 g fresh prawns
1 tsp minced garlic
1 Tbsp finely chopped spring onion
1 Tbsp freshly chopped coriander
1 egg-white, lightly beaten

2 tsp fish sauce
freshly ground black pepper
1 baguette, cut diagonally
* into 15mm slices*
oil for deep frying

Shell and de-vein the prawns and chop finely. Combine the prawn, garlic, onion, coriander, egg-white, fish sauce and pepper to produce a thick, coarse paste, then spread evenly over the slices of baguette.

Heat the oil until it starts to smoke, then lower heat slightly and gently add the baguette slices with the paste side down. Cook for 1-2 minutes, until golden brown and crispy.

Remove and drain on kitchen paper, then serve immediately.

CHAO TOM (shrimp paste on sugar cane): BANH MI CHIEN (prawn toast)

BAKWAN UDANG (prawn fritters)   *Indonesia*

200 g fresh baby shrimps
2 Tbsp finely chopped shallot
2 tsp finely chopped ginger
1 tsp minced garlic
75 g chopped leek

oil for deep frying
100 g plain flour
0.25 tsp salt
2 fresh eggs
freshly ground black pepper

Shell and de-vein the shrimps. Heat 2 Tbsp oil in a pan and sauté the shrimps for 2 minutes, then remove and drain on kitchen paper.

Clean the pan, add a little more oil and sauté the shallot, ginger and garlic for 2 minutes. Add the leek and continue to cook for a further 2-3 minutes, then remove and drain off excess oil.

Sift the flour and salt into a bowl and make a well in the centre. Break in the eggs and beat to produce a smooth batter, using a little water if necessary. Add the shrimps and vegetables, season with pepper and stir to blend.

Heat the remaining oil in a wok until it starts to smoke, then drop in spoonfuls of the batter and fry until golden and crispy. Remove with a slotted spoon and drain on kitchen paper, then serve with a chilli-vinegar dip.

KADUKA ERAL (mustard prawns)   *India*

600 g fresh prawns
2 Tbsp vegetable oil
1 Tbsp mustard seeds
8 curry leaves
1 large onion, finely chopped
2 tsp finely chopped garlic
2 tomatoes, skinned and chopped
1 Tbsp chilli powder
salt to taste
freshly chopped coriander
small green chillies

Shell and de-vein the prawns, leaving the tails intact.

Heat the oil until very hot, then add the mustard seeds and curry leaves. When the seeds start to crackle lower heat slightly, add the onion and garlic and sauté until soft, then add the tomato and stir for a further 5 minutes

Add the prawns and chilli powder and cook over a moderate heat for 5 minutes, stirring frequently, then add salt to taste.

Transfer to a serving dish and garnish with freshly chopped coriander and small green chillies.

GAMBAS (shrimps in chilli-garlic sauce)   *Philippines*

400 g fresh shrimps
2 Tbsp fresh calamansi juice
sea salt to taste
freshly ground black pepper

1 tsp sweet paprika
100 ml olive oil
1.5 Tbsp minced garlic
1 Tbsp finely chopped red chilli

Shell and de-vein the shrimps and wash in calamansi juice, then drain and season with salt, pepper and paprika.

Heat the oil and sauté the garlic for 2 minutes, then increase heat to high, add the shrimps and chilli and cook for 45 seconds.

Adjust seasonings to taste, then remove with a slotted spoon and transfer to a warm serving dish.

CHEMEEN OOLARTHIATHU (spicy prawns) — *India*

600 g fresh prawns
1 tsp ground turmeric
1 tsp salt
2 Tbsp fresh lemon juice
oil for deep frying
6 curry leaves
2 onions, finely chopped
6 cloves garlic, finely chopped
3 tomatoes, skinned & chopped

1 tsp ground coriander
1 tsp freshly ground black pepper
freshly chopped coriander leaves

Batter:
2 Tbsp cornflour
1 Tbsp superfine flour
2 eggs
1.5 Tbsp red chilli paste

Shell and de-vein the prawns, sprinkle with turmeric, salt and lemon juice and set aside for 30 minutes, then dip into the prepared batter.

Heat the oil in a pan and deep-fry the prawns until they are golden and crispy, then remove with a slotted spoon and drain on kitchen paper.

Heat a small quantity of oil in a fresh pan and add the curry leaves. When they start to crackle add the onion and garlic and sauté for 3-4 minutes, then add the tomato, coriander and pepper and continue to stir for a further 5 minutes.

Add the prawns and toss to coat evenly. Cook for a further minute, then transfer to a serving dish and garnish with freshly chopped coriander.

To make the batter, sift both the flours into a bowl, then break in the eggs and add the chilli paste. pour in just sufficient cold water to produce a thick batter and mix until smooth.

POO JA (stuffed crab shells)   *Thailand*

4 medium-size crabs
125 g minced lean pork
1 small onion, finely chopped
2.5 cm knob ginger, finely chopped
2 tsp minced garlic
1 tsp chopped coriander root
1.5 Tbsp cornflour

125 ml thick coconut milk
1 egg, lightly whisked
salt to taste
freshly ground black pepper
oil for deep frying
fresh corinader leaves

Cook the crabs in rapidly boiling water, then allow to cool. Remove the back shells and wash in salted water, then set aside in a warming oven.

Extract all the meat from the crabs, shred finely and place in a bowl. Add the pork, onion, ginger, garlic, coriander root, cornflour, coconut milk and egg and season to taste with salt and pepper. Mix to blend thoroughly, then place in the reserved shells and cook in a steamer for 20 minutes. Set aside to cool.

Heat the oil in a wok until it starts to smoke, then lower heat slightly and deep-fry the crab shells until the tops are crispy and golden.

Transfer to a serving dish and garnish with coriander leaves. Serve immediately.

ZHA XIE QIAN (deep-fried crab claws)   *Singapore*

8 fresh crab claws
150 g fresh shrimp
75 g fat pork
1 egg white
1 tsp sugar
0.5 tsp freshly ground white pepper
1 Tbsp light soy sauce
1 tsp dark soy sauce
2 tsp Chinese wine
1 tsp sesame oil
1.5 Tbsp cornflour
vegetable oil for frying

Crack the claws and cook in a steamer for 10 minutes, then carefully remove the shell, leaving the meat intact and still attached to the 'nipper'. Shell and de-vein the shrimps and, together with the pork, pass through a mincer.

Beat the egg-white lightly in a bowl and add the shrimp, sugar, pepper, soy sauce, wine, sesame oil and half the cornflour. Blend well, adding a little cold water if necessary, to produce a thick, sticky paste.

Mould a portion of mixture around each crab claw and dust with the remaining cornflour. Heat the oil in a wok until it starts to smoke, then lower heat slightly and deep-fry the claws until golden and crispy. Drain well before serving.

POO MAN PLA (crab cakes)   *Thailand*

225 g crabmeat
2 tsp hot chilli paste
2 tsp light soy sauce
75 ml thick coconut milk
1 egg, lightly beaten with
  1 Tbsp cornflour

75 g green beans, finely chopped
salt to taste
freshly ground black pepper
oil for frying
75 ml chilli sauce

Flake the crabmeat and place in a bowl. Add the chilli paste, soy sauce, coconut milk and egg and mix well.

Add the beans and season to taste with salt and pepper and combine thoroughly, then shape into small cakes, about 5 cm in diameter, and chill for 1 hour.

Heat the oil in a shallow pan and fry the fish cakes, turning once, until crispy and golden, then transfer to a serving plate and top with hot chilli sauce.

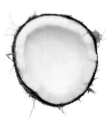

CHONG YOU BING (onion cakes) — *Singapore*

250 g plain flour
75 g lard
1 tsp sugar
0,25 tsp salt
0.25 tsp freshly ground pepper

0.25 tsp Chinese five-spice powder
2 Tbsp sesame oil
8 spring onions, finely chopped
egg wash
3 Tbsp vegetable oil

Sift the flour into a mixing bowl and add just sufficient boiling water to produce a thick, sticky dough, then cover with a cloth and set aside for 20 minutes. Add lard, sugar, salt, pepper, five-spice powder and half the sesame oil and knead firmly for 5 minutes, then roll out on a lightly-floured surface.

Cover evenly with the spring onion and sprinkle remaining sesame oil on top. Shape into a roll, 5 cm in diameter, then cut into 2 cm slices and flatten slightly. Brush with egg wash and cook in a steamer for 10 minutes, then leave to cool.

Heat the oil until it starts to smoke, then lower heat slightly and fry the onion cakes for 2-3 minutes, turning once, until golden-brown and crispy.

WOO KOK (fried taro dumplings) — *Hong Kong*

3 dried Chinese mushrooms
400 g taro root
150 g fresh shrimps
100 g lean pork, chopped
vegetable oil for frying

2 tsp fish sauce
freshly ground black pepper
1 baguette, cut diagonally
 into 15mm slices
oil for deep frying

Soak the mushrooms in warm water for 20 minutes, then discard the hard stems and dice the caps. Peel and slice the taro and cook in a double boiler until tender, then allow to cool and mash. Shell and de-vein the shrimps and pass through a coarse mincer together with the pork.

Heat 2 Tbsp oil in a wok and stir-fry the shrimp mixture for 3 minutes, then add the diced mushroom and season to taste with salt and pepper. Mix the cornflour with a small quantity of cold water and add to the wok. Continue to cook for a further 2-3 minutes, stirring frequently, then remove and drain on kitchen paper.

Sift the flour into a bowl, add the melted lard and mashed taro and knead firmly, then turn on to a lightly-floured surface and shape into a roll. Cut the roll into slices and spoon a portion of the shrimp mixture on top, then fold and pinch the edges, securing with a little iced water.

Heat the remaining oil until it starts to smoke, then lower heat slightly and deep-fry the taro dumplings until golden and crispy.

TSUEN GUEN (spring rolls)　　　*Hong Kong*

2 dried Chinese mushrooms
1 tsp salt
1 Tbsp sugar
vegetable oil for deep frying
125 g fresh baby shrimps
125 g bamboo shoots, shredded
150 g bean sprouts, blanched
125 g roasted pork, shredded

2 Tbsp Chinese wine
1 Tbsp light soy sauce
1 tsp dark soy sauce
1 tsp sesame oil
0.5 tsp freshly ground white pepper
2 tsp cornflour
12 spring roll wrappers
egg-wash

Soak the mushrooms in warm water for 40 minutes, then discard the hard stems. Shred the caps and place in a heat-proof bowl. Add the salt, 1 tsp of sugar and 1 Tbsp of oil and steam for 15 minutes. Shell and de-vein the shrimps.

Heat 4 Tbsp oil in a wok, add the mushroom and bamboo shoot and stir-fry over a high heat for 1 minute. Add the bean sprouts, pork, shrimps, wine, soy sauce, sesame oil and remaining sugar and stir for a further 2 minutes. Mix the corn-flour with a little cold water and stir into the mixture, then leave to cool.

Lay the wrappers on a lightly-greased surface and add portions of the mixture. Fold a corner of each wrapper over the mixture, then fold in each side and roll up tightly. Brush with egg-wash.

Heat the remaining oil in a wok until it starts to smoke, then lower heat slightly and deep-fry the rolls until golden and crispy. Remove and drain.

GAI HAW BAI TOEY (chicken in pandan leaves) *Thailand*

3 boneless chicken thighs
2 shallots, finely chopped
1 Tbsp finely chopped ginger
2 tsp minced garlic
1 tsp finely chopped coriander root
1 tsp finely chopped lemon grass
6 black peppercorns
0.5 tsp salt
2 Tbsp chilli sauce
1 Tbsp dark soy sauce
2 Tbsp Worcestershire sauce
150 ml thick coconut milk
2 tsp palm sugar
fresh pandan leaves
oil for deep frying

Remove the skin from the chicken thighs and cut the meat into bite-size cubes. Place the shallot, ginger, garlic, coriander, lemon grass, peppercorns, salt and 2-3 Tbsp cold water in a mortar and pound to produce a smooth paste.

Transfer paste to a dish, add the chilli sauce, soy sauce, coconut milk and palm sugar and stir to blend thoroughly, then add the chicken. Leave to marinate for 30 minutes, then wrap the pieces of chicken in pandan leaves (see glossary).

Heat the oil in a wok until it starts to smoke, then lower heat slightly and deep-fry the chicken 'parcels' until tender, approximately 10 minutes. Remove with a slotted spoon and transfer to a platter, then unwrap and serve with a side dish of hot and sour sauce

YOW GAI (drunken chicken) *Hong Kong*

1.5 kilo chicken
25 mm knob fresh ginger, sliced
2 spring onions, sliced
chicken stock

2 tsp dark soy sauce
2 tsp sugar
salt and white pepper to taste
300 ml Chinese wine

Place the chicken in a large pot, add the ginger and spring onions and pour in sufficient stock to cover the chicken by 15 mm. Bring to the boil, then add the soy sauce, sugar and turmeric.

Lower heat and simmer until the chicken is tender, then remove, chop into bite-size pieces and place in a dish. Season to taste with salt and pepper.

Combine 175 ml of the stock with the wine and pour over the chicken, then cover with foil and place in the refrigerator for 24 hours, turning occasionally.

MURG PAKORAS (chicken nuggets in batter) *India*

2 boneless chicken breasts
1 Tbsp finely chopped ginger
1 tsp finely chopped garlic
2 cloves
2 black cardamom seeds
0.5 tsp cumin seeds
0.5 tsp coriander seeds
300 g natural yoghurt
salt and white pepper to taste

oil for deep frying

Batter:
200 g chick pea flour
large pinch of salt
2 eggs
0.25 tsp ground cumin
0.25 tsp poppy seeds
1 Tbsp fresh lemon juice

Remove the skin from the chicken breasts and slice the meat into bite-size pieces. Place in a shallow dish and season with salt and pepper.

Grind together the ginger, garlic, cloves, cardamoms, cumin and coriander seeds and mix with the yoghurt. Pour mixture over the chicken and place in refrigerator to marinate for 6 hours, then remove and dip into prepared batter.

Heat the oil in a wok until very hot and deep-fry the chicken pieces until golden and crispy, then remove with a slotted spoon, drain off excess oil and transfer to a warm platter. Serve immediately with sweet mango chutney.

To make the batter, sift the flour and salt into a mixing bowl and break in the eggs. Stir well, then add the remaining ingredients and blend thoroughly until thick and smooth.

SATAY (kebabs with peanut sauce) — *Malaysia*

200 g boneless chicken breasts
200 g lamb or mutton
200 g rump steak

Marinade:
4 shallots, finely chopped
2 fresh red chillies, finely chopped
2 tsp finely chopped lemon grass
1 tsp finely chopped garlic
1 tsp ground cumin
1 tsp ground coriander
2 tsp soft brown sugar
0.5 tsp salt
2 Tbsp fresh lime juice
2 tsp peanut oil
150 ml thick coconut milk

Sauce:
200 g roasted peanuts
4 shallots, chopped
6 fresh red chillies, chopped
2 tsp chopped ginger
1 tsp chopped garlic
2 tsp chopped lemon grass
2 candlenuts, chopped
1 tsp ground cumin
1 tsp ground coriander
1 tsp ground turmeric
0.5 tsp ground cinnamon
2 Tbsp peanut oil
1 Tbsp soft brown sugar
salt to taste

Slice the meat into bite-size pieces and place in a shallow bowl. Combine all the marinade ingredients and pour over the meat. Stir to coat evenly and set aside for at least 4 hours (preferably refrigerate overnight).

Thread the marinated meats on to wooden skewers (3-4 pieces for each skewer) and cook over very hot charcoal, turning frequently, for 4-5 minutes. Serve with packets of compressed sticky rice, slices of cucumber and a bowl of satay sauce for dipping.

To make the sauce, shell and skin the peanuts and grind to a fine powder. Place the shallot, chilli, ginger, garlic, lemon grass, candlenut and spices in a mortar, add just sufficient water to produce a thick paste and pound until smooth.

Heat the oil in a wok and stir-fry the spice-paste for 5 minutes, then add the sugar, salt and 450 ml cold water. Bring to the boil, then add the ground peanut and cook for 8-10 minutes, stirring frequently, until the sauce thickens. Allow to cool slightly before serving.

SHAMI KEBABS (lamb & lentil patties)   *Pakistan*

400 g fresh lean lamb
100 g red lentils
4 Tbsp ghee
1 tsp ground coriander
1 tsp ground cumin

2 Tbsp garam masala
1 tsp salt
0.5 tsp freshly ground black pepper
3 eggs, lightly beaten

Pass the lamb through a coarse mincer. Wash the lentils under cold running water, then drain, add to the meat, and stir well.

Heat half the ghee in a frying pan and cook the meat over a moderate heat for 7-8 minutes, stirring frequently, then add the coriander, cumin, garam masala, salt and pepper and stir for a further minute.

Remove from heat and allow mixture to cool, then pass through a fine mincer into a clean bowl. Break in the eggs and stir to blend thoroughly, then divide the mixture and shape into small patties, approximately 15 mm thick. Place in the refrigerator for 1 hour.

Heat remaining ghee in a clean frying pan and cook the patties for 3-4 minutes, turning once, until outsides are golden and crispy. Serve immediately with a side dish of mint chutney

SHEEK KEBABS (barbecued minced lamb)   *Pakistan*

400 g minced lean lamb
2 onions, finely chopped
4 green chillies, finely chopped
1 Tbsp finely chopped fresh ginger
2 tsp minced garlic

1 tsp ground coriander
1 tsp ground cumin
1 Tbsp garam masala
salt to taste
2 Tbsp fresh lime juice

Chop the meat and place through a fine mincer together with the onion. Add all the remaining ingredients and mix thoroughly, add just sufficient cold water to produce a thick sticky paste.

Mould the paste around wooden skewers (the kebabs should be approximately 10 cm long) and cook over hot charcoal for 4-6 minutes, turning occasionally.

Carefully remove the meat from the skewers and serve with a side dish of mint chutney.

SHAMI KEBAB (lamb & lentil patties), **SHEEK KEBAB** (minced lamb) and **GOSHT TIKKA** (lamb nuggets)

GOSHT TIKKA (barbecued spicy lamb nuggets) *Pakistan*

400g boned lamb shoulder
250 g natural yoghurt
2 tsp ground coriander
2 tsp ground cumin
2 tsp red chilli powder

1 tsp ground anise
1 Tbsp garam masala
0.5 tsp salt
2 Tbsp fresh lime juice

Cut the lamb into bite-size chunks and place in a shallow dish. Mix the yoghurt with the remaining ingredients and pour over the meat. Stir to ensure the meat is evenly coated, then place in the refrigerator for 6 hours, stirring occasionally.

Thread the marinated meat on to skewers and barbecue over hot charcoal for 8-10 minutes, turning frequently, then remove meat from the skewers and serve with a side dish of sweet chutney.

KARI PAP (curry pasties)   *Malaysia*

vegetable oil for frying
375 g minced beef
2 potatoes, parboiled and diced
1 onion, finely chopped
2 tsp finely chopped fresh red chilli
2 tsp finely chopped fresh ginger
1 tsp minced garlic
0.5 tsp finely chopped lemon grass
1 Tbsp curry powder
0.25 tsp ground turmeric
8 cm cinnamon stick
125 ml thick coconut milk
salt and pepper to taste
350 g puff pastry

Heat a little oil in a pan and sauté the onion for 3 minutes, then add the chilli, ginger, garlic and lemon grass and stir for a further 2 minutes.

Add the beef, curry, turmeric, cinnamon and coconut milk and bring to the boil, then add the potato and simmer until the liquid has been almost absorbed. Remove mixture and set aside to cool. Discard the cinnamon stick.

Roll out the pastry and cut into 7 cm circles. Spoon a little of the mixture on the centre of each pastry round, then fold over to form half-moons and flute the edges to seal securely.

Heat oil in a deep pan until it starts to smoke and fry the pasties until golden, then remove and drain on kitchen paper before transferring to serving platter.

SAMBAL DAGING (shredded beef)   *Malaysia*

400 g lean beef
1 Tbsp shredded ginger
1 Tbsp finely shredded red chilli
4 shallots, finely shredded

2 Tbsp vegetable oil
200 g thick coconut milk
1 Tbsp tamarind water
2 tsp sugar

Cut the beef into chunks and boil until tender, then allow to cool and shred. Pound together the ginger, chilli and half the shallot to produce a smooth paste.

Heat the oil in a pan and sauté the remaining shallot until crispy, then remove and set aside. Add the spice paste to the pan and stir for 2-3 minutes, then add meat, coconut milk, tamarind water and sugar and bring to the boil.

Cook over a moderate heat until the liquid has been absorbed, then add reserved shallot, adjust seasonings to taste and stir to combine. Allow to cool and transfer to a serving dish.

CUTLIS (meatballs)   *Sri Lanka*

300 g lean minced beef
1.5 Tbsp vinegar
1 tsp salt
0.5 tsp freshly ground black pepper
vegetable oil for deep frying
1 onion, finely chopped
2 tsp minced garlic

2 sticks celery, finely chopped
3 fresh red chillies, finely chopped
2 tsp finely chopped fresh mint
300 g potatoes, boiled and mashed
egg wash
75 g white breadcrumbs

Season the beef with vinegar, salt and pepper and set aside for 30 minutes. Heat 2 Tbsp oil in a pan and stir-fry the beef for 3-4 minutes, then remove and drain on kitchen paper.

Add a little extra oil to the pan, re-heat and add the onion and garlic. Sauté for 3 minutes, then replace the meat, add the celery, chilli and mint and continue to stir over a moderate heat for a further 3-4 minutes. Add the potato and stir to blend thoroughly, then remove pan from the heat and allow to cool.

Divide the mixture, shape into balls (or croquettes and patties) and place in the refrigerator for 1 hour, then brush with egg wash and coat with breadcrumbs.

Heat remaining oil until it starts to smoke, then lower heat slightly and deep-fry the meatballs, until golden. Remove with a slotted spoon and drain on kitchen paper, then serve immediately.

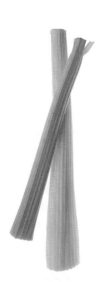

CHA SHUI (barbecued pork)   *Hong Kong*

750 g boned pork loin, with skin
2 tsp course salt
2 tsp finely chopped ginger
1 tsp finely chopped garlic
2 Tbsp soft brown sugar

2 Tbsp Chinese wine
2 Tbsp light soy sauce
0.25 tsp red food colouring
125 g clear honey

Score the pork skin with a sharp knife and rub in the salt, then cut the meat into 4 cm strips. Combine the ginger, garlic, sugar, wine, soy sauce and colouring and rub into the underside of the loin. Set aside for 1 hour, then thread on skewers and coat with honey.

Cook over a very hot charcoal fire for 25-30 minutes, turning frequently and basting occasionally with remaining honey. Allow to cool slightly, then cut into thin strips.

CHA SHUI BAO (pork filled steamed buns)   *Hong Kong*

2 Tbsp vegetable oil
3 spring onions, finely chopped
225 g barbecued pork, chopped
2 Tbsp oyster sauce
1 Tbsp light soy sauce
2 tsp sugar
1 tsp freshly ground black pepper

2 Tbsp chicken stock
2 tsp cornflour

Dough:
2 Tbsp sugar
2 tsp dried yeast
450 g plain flour
0.25 tsp salt

Heat the oil in a pan and stir-fry the onion for 2 minutes, then add the pork, soy sauce, oyster sauce, sugar, pepper and stock. Bring to the boil and cook for 3 minutes, stirring frequently. Mix the cornflour with a small quantity of cold water and stir into the mixture, then remove pan from heat and allow to cool.

Spoon small quantities on to pieces of dough and fold up edges to form buns, leaving small openings at the top. Arrange in a bamboo basket, cover and steam over rapidly-boiling water for 10-12 minutes.

To make the dough, dissolve the sugar in 100 ml warm water, then stir in the yeast and allow to ferment for 12-15 minutes. Sift the flour and salt into a bowl, make a well and add the fermented yeast. Mix with a wooden spoon, then knead firmly for 10 minutes. Turn on to a lightly-floured surface and shape into a roll, 5 cm in diameter, then cut into 2.5 cm slices and flatten slightly with the hands.

ZHA ROU JUAN (stir-fried pork rolls) — *China*

300 g pork fillet
0.5 tsp salt
1 Tbsp cornflour
1 tsp sesame oil
3 flat mushrooms, shredded
3 sticks celery, shredded
2 Tbsp chopped walnuts

egg-wash
3 Tbsp vegetable oil
2 tsp chopped ginger
1 tsp chopped garlic
3 Tbsp chicken stock
2 tsp light soy sauce
2 tsp sugar

Cut the pork into very thin slices and place in a shallow dish. Sprinkle on the salt, cornflour and sesame oil and set aside for 20 minutes.

Blanch the mushroom and celery and lay a piece of each on top of a slice of pork. Add a little chopped walnut, then roll up and seal with egg-wash.

Heat 2 Tbsp oil in a wok, fry the pork rolls until cooked to liking, then remove and drain on kitchen paper. Add remaining oil and re-heat, then add the ginger and garlic and stir-fry for 2 minutes.

Replace the pork rolls, add the stock, soy sauce and sugar and bring to the boil, then lower heat and stir for a further minute. Transfer to a platter and serve with plum sauce.

Soups & Salads

SOTO AYAM (spicy chicken soup), *recipe page 45*

BUN NUOC LEO (shrimp soup with noodles)   *Vietnam*

350 g fresh shrimps
300 g vermicelli noodles
2 shallots
2 cloves garlic
1 fresh red chilli
2 bulbs lemon grass
1 tsp curry powder
2 Tbsp vegetable oil

0.5 tsp sugar
2 tsp oyster sauce
3 Tbsp thick coconut milk
1 litre fish stock
fish sauce to taste
freshly ground white pepper
fresh coriander leaves

Shell and de-vein the shrimps and cut in half lengthways. Soak the noodles in cold water and set aside for 20 minutes. Finely chop the shallots, garlic, chilli and lemon grass and pound together with the curry powder and a small quantity of cold water to produce a smooth paste.

Heat the oil in a pan and stir-fry the spice-paste for 2-3 minutes, then add the shrimps, sugar, oyster sauce, coconut milk and stock and bring to the boil. Lower heat and allow to simmer for 5 minutes, stirring frequently, then season to taste with fish sauce and freshly ground pepper.

Meanwhile drain the noodles and cook in boiling water for 1-2 minutes, until tender, then drain in a colander. Transfer the noodles to individual soup bowls and ladle in the soup, then garnish with fresh coriander leaves.

GAENG SOM GOONG (spicy prawn soup) — *Thailand*

400 g fresh prawns
6 red chillies, seeded and chopped
4 shallots, finely chopped
1 Tbsp finely chopped ginger
2 tsp minced garlic
2 tsp finely chopped lemon grass
0.5 tsp grated kaffir lime rind
1 tsp crumbled shrimp paste
1 tsp ground turmeric

1.5 litres clear fish stock
1 small green papaya, thinly sliced
125 g winged beans
100 g baby corn, trimmed
3 Tbsp palm sugar
1.5 Tbsp fish sauce
2 Tbsp tamarind water
1 sprig kaffir lime leaves

Shell and de-vein one third of the prawns and place through a fine mincer. Shell and de-vein the remaining prawns, leaving tails attached.

Place the chilli, ginger, garlic, lemon grass, lime rind, shrimp paste and turmeric in a mortar and pound to produce a smooth paste. Add the minced prawn and blend thoroughly.

In a saucepan, bring the stock to the boil, then stir in the spice paste and cook for 2 minutes. Add the papaya, beans, corn, sugar, fish sauce and tamarind water and allow to simmer for 5 minutes.

Finally, add the prawns and cook for a further 1-2 minutes, then transfer to a soup tureen and float the lime leaves on top.

HAI YUK SUK MAI GUNG
(crabmeat & sweetcorn soup)

Hong Kong

250 g cooked crabmeat
salt & pepper
2 Tbsp Chinese wine
1 tsp dark soy sauce
1 tsp sesame oil

1 Tbsp cornflour
1.5 litres chicken stock
250 g can sweetcorn, drained
2 eggs, lightly beaten

Flake the crabmeat, season with salt and pepper and place in a shallow dish. Mix together the wine, soy sauce, sesame oil and half the cornflour and pour over the crabmeat, then set aside for 20 minutes.

Pour the stock into a saucepan, add the corn and bring slowly to the boil, then lower heat and allow to simmer for 3-4 minutes. Add the crabmeat, bring back to the boil and cook for a further minute. Mix the remaining cornflour with a small quantity of cold water and stir into the soup to thicken slightly.

Pour the egg into the soup slowly and stir continuously until it starts to set in threads, then transfer to a soup tureen and serve immediately.

HOI SIN DOU FU GUNG
(seafood & beancurd soup)

Hong Kong

125 g fresh cuttlefish
1 Tbsp fresh lemon juice
125 g fresh shrimps
125 g fish fillet, sliced
1 egg, lightly beaten
1 Tbsp light soy sauce
1 tsp sesame oil

2 Tbsp cornflour
1.5 litres stock
150 g cabbage, shredded
2 tsp finely chopped fresh ginger
225 g fresh beancurd,
*   cut into bite-size pieces*
2 spring onions, sliced

Clean the cuttlefish, remove ink sac and slice thinly then sprinkle with lemon juice and set aside for 10 minutes. Shell and de-vein the shrimps and place in a bowl together with the fish and cuttlefish. Mix the egg, soy sauce, sesame oil, pepper and 2 tsp cornflour. Pour over the seafood and set aside for 15 minutes.

Pour the stock into a saucepan and bring to the boil. Add the seafood, cabbage and ginger and cook for 2 minutes, then lower heat, add the beancurd and allow to simmer for a further 5-6 minutes.

Add the spring onion and adjust seasonings to taste. Mix the remaining cornflour with a small quantity of cold water and stir into the soup to thicken, then remove from heat and stir in the wine. Transfer to a soup tureen and serve immediately.

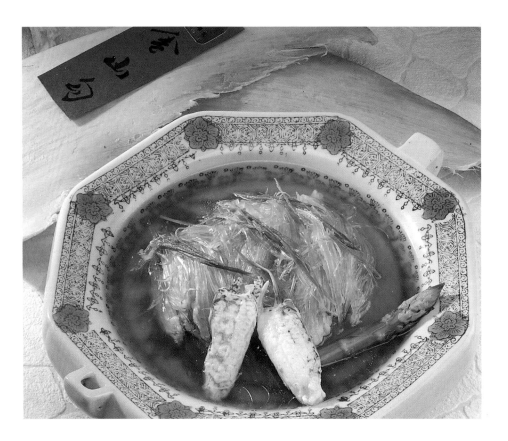

XIE ROU YU CHI (shark's fin and crabmeat soup) — *China*

450 g shark's fin
2 spring onions, sliced
25 mm knob fresh ginger, sliced
2 Tbsp Chinese wine
2 Tbsp finely shredded Yunan ham
1.5 litres superior chicken stock

4 crab claws
4 small asparagus spears
1 Tbsp light soy sauce
1 tsp dark soy sauce
0.5 tsp freshly ground white pepper

Place the shark's fin in a pan and add sufficient cold water to cover. Soak for 12 hours, then transfer to a pan of boiling water and add the onion, ginger and wine. Lower heat and allow to simmer for 5-6 hours, then remove pan from heat, cover and allow to stand for 1 hour.

Drain the shark's fin and transfer to a large tureen, then sprinkle the ham on top. Bring the stock to the boil and pour into the tureen, then cover, place on a rack and steam over rapidly boiling water for 45 minutes.

Meanwhile, crack the crab claws and steam for 10 minutes, then carefully remove shells, leaving the meat in one piece. Cook the asparagus until tender, then cut each spear in half. Add both to the tureen, season with soy sauce and pepper and continue to steam for a further 5 minutes, then serve immediately.

MALU HODHI (spicy fish soup)   *Sri Lanka*

300 g white fish fillets, sliced
2 onions, chopped
75 g lentils
3 fresh red chillies, finely chopped
2 tsp finely chopped ginger
1 tsp minced garlic

4 curry leaves
0.5 tsp ground coriander
0.5 tsp ground cumin
0.5 tsp white peppercorns
1 Tbsp ghee
2 tsp fresh lime juice

Place the fish in a large pan, add the lentils, chilli, ginger, garlic, curry leaves, half the onion and 1.5 litres water and bring to the boil.

Cover the pan and cook over a moderate heat for 20 minutes, then remove the lid, add the coriander, cumin and pepper and simmer for a further 20 minutes.

Pour the liquid through a fine strainer into a fresh pan. Flake the fish and add a little to the pan.

Meanwhile, heat the ghee and stir-fry the remaining onion for 4-5 minutes, then remove, drain off excess oil and add to soup.

Bring the soup back to the boil, adjust seasonings to taste and transfer to a tureen. Sprinkle the lemon juice on top and serve immediately.

SHENG YU TANG (RAW FISH SOUP)   *Taiwan*

350 g white fish fillets
1 Tbsp olive oil
2 shallots, thinly sliced
1 Tbsp finely chopped fresh ginger
4 lettuce leaves, shredded
0.5 tsp sesame oil
1 litre fish stock
salt to taste
freshly ground white pepper
freshly chopped coriander

Remove the skin from the fish fillets, ensure no small bones remain, and cut the meat into thin slices.

Heat the oil in a small pan and sauté the shallot and ginger for 2-3 minutes, then remove and drain on kitchen paper.

Place the shredded lettuce in the bottom of a soup tureen, then add the shallot, ginger and fish and sprinkle with sesame oil.

Bring the stock to the boil and season with salt and pepper, then pour over the fish and garnish with freshly chopped coriander. Serve immediately.

41

TAMATAR KA SHORBA (spicy tomato soup)　　*India*

1.5 kilos ripe tomatoes, quartered
1 Tbsp finely chopped ginger
1 Tbsp roasted coriander seeds
0.5 tsp ground turmeric
6 curry leaves
salt to taste
6 fresh red chillies, finely chopped
2 tsp finely chopped garlic
2 Tbsp vegetable oil
1 tsp cumin seeds
1 tsp mustard seeds
garlic croutons

Place the tomato, ginger, coriander, turmeric and 3 curry leaves in a saucepan, add 1.5 litres water and bring to the boil. Lower heat and allow to simmer for 30 minutes, then strain through a fine sieve into a fresh saucepan. Return to a moderate heat, add salt to taste and continue to simmer for a further 10 minutes.

Heat the oil in a small pan and add the cumin seeds, mustard seeds, chilli, garlic and remaining curry leaves Stir until the seeds start to crackle, then add to the soup. Stir well and cook for a further minute, then transfer to a soup tureen and sprinkle garlic croutons on top.

DAHI KA SHORBA (yoghurt soup)　　*India*

800 g natural yoghurt
3 Tbsp butter
1 tsp cumin seeds
1 small onion, finely chopped
1 small tomato,
　skinned, seeded and chopped

1 tsp finely chopped ginger
1 tsp finely chopped green chilli
0.5 tsp ground turmeric
75 ml single cream
salt & freshly ground black pepper
1 Tbsp freshly chopped coriander

Whisk the yoghurt. Melt the butter in a pan and add cumin seeds. Stir over a moderate heat until the seeds start to crackle, then add the onion, tomato, ginger, chilli and turmeric and stir for 2 minutes.

Remove pan from the heat and allow to cool slightly, then return to a moderate heat, add the yoghurt, cream and coriander. Bring to the boil, then remove from heat, stir in remaining cream and adjust seasonings to taste.

Transfer to soup cups, garnish with coriander leaves and serve immediately.

SUAN LA TANG (hot & sour soup) *Taiwan*

4 dried Chinese mushrooms
150 g fresh shrimps
2 Tbsp vegetable oil
125 g roasted pork, shredded
75 g bamboo shoot, shredded
75 g cucumber, shredded
4 fresh red chillies, finely chopped
25 mm fresh ginger, finely chopped
100 g fresh beancurd, diced

1.5 litres chicken stock
2 tsp light soy sauce
1 tsp dark soy sauce
1 Tbsp Chinese wine
1 Tbsp vinegar
1 tsp freshly ground white pepper
2 tsp cornflour
1 egg, lightly beaten
1 tsp chilli oil

Soak the mushrooms in warm water for 20 minutes, then discard the hard stems and shred the caps. Shell and de-vein the shrimps and cut in half, lengthways.

Heat the oil in a large pan, add the mushroom, shrimp, pork, bamboo shoot, cucumber, chilli, ginger and beancurd and stir-fry for 2 minutes, then pour in the stock and bring to the boil.

Continue to boil for 1 minute, then lower heat, add soy sauce, wine, vinegar and pepper and allow to simmer for a further 3-4 minutes.

Mix the cornflour with a small quantity of cold water and stir into the soup to thicken slightly. Add the egg and stir until it starts to set in thin shreds, then transfer to a soup tureen. Finally, heat the chilli oil and sprinkle over the soup.

DONG GUA TONG (winter melon soup)   *Hong Kong*

500 g winter melon
6 dried Chinese mushrooms
4 water chestnuts
125 g fresh shrimps
1 Tbsp vegetable oil
1 Tbsp finely chopped shallot
2 tsp finely chopped ginger
1 tsp minced garlic
125 g fresh pork, diced
125 g chicken breast, chopped
125 duck breast, chopped
1.75 litres chicken stock
1 Tbsp Chinese wine
1 Tbsp light soy sauce
1 tsp freshly ground black pepper
75 g crabmeat, flaked
2 spring onions, finely chopped
1 tsp sesame oil
1 Tbsp finely shredded Yunan ham

Square the bottom of the melon so that it will stand upright. Slice off the top quarter (and retain) and scoop out the seeds and sufficient flesh to allow space for the stock to be added.

Soak the mushrooms in warm water for 20 minutes, then discard the stems and cut the caps into fine strips. Peel and finely chop the water chestnuts. Shell and de-vein the shrimps.

Heat the oil in a saucepan and sauté the shallot, ginger and garlic for 2 minutes, then add the pork, chicken and duck and cook for a further minute. Pour in the stock and bring to the boil, then add the wine, soy sauce and pepper and allow to simmer for 10 minutes.

Transfer the stock to the melon, cover with the top quarter and place in a steamer. Cook over gently boiling water for 2-3 hours, then add the shrimps, crabmeat and spring onion and cook for a further 10 minutes.

To serve, scoop out the flesh from the sides of the melon and place in individual soup bowls, then pour in the stock. Heat the sesame oil and sprinkle on top, then garnish with finely shredded Yunan ham.

SOTO AYAM (spicy chicken soup)   *Indonesia*

1 chicken, approx. 1.25 kilos
1 large onion, coarsely chopped
25 mm knob fresh ginger, sliced
2 stalks lemon grass, chopped
2 curry leaves
1 tsp salt
1 tsp freshly ground black pepper
4 shallots, finely chopped

1 tsp finely chopped garlic
3 fresh red chillies, finely chopped
1 tsp crumbled shrimp paste
3 Tbsp peanut oil
0.5 tsp ground coriander
0.5 tsp ground turmeric
75 g bean sprouts
freshly chopped parsley

Joint the chicken and place in a large saucepan together with the onion, ginger, lemon grass, curry leaves, salt and pepper. Cover with 2 litres cold water and bring to the boil, then cover the pan, lower heat and allow to simmer until the chicken is tender, approximately 1 hour.

Place the shallot, garlic, chilli and shrimp paste in a mortar and pound to produce a smooth paste. Heat the oil in a fresh saucepan and stir-fry the spice-paste for 2 minutes, then add the coriander and turmeric and cook for a further minute. Pour in the stock through a fine strainer and adjust seasonings to taste.

Meanwhile, blanch the bean sprouts in boiling water, then drain in a colander and arrange in the bottom of individual soup bowls. Ladle the stock over the bean sprouts and garnish with freshly chopped parsley.

CHONG AO JI GAN (Chicken Liver & Ginger Soup) *Singapore*

4 dried Chinese mushrooms
225 g chicken livers
75 g chicken giblets
2 cloves garlic, chopped
10 black peppercorns
30 mm knob ginger, finely sliced

2 Tbsp peanut oil
1 Tbsp Chinese wine
1 Tbsp light soy sauce
2 tsp dark soy sauce
2 tsp sesame oil
fresh basil leaves

Soak the mushrooms in warm water for 40 minutes, then discard the stems and cut the caps into fine strips.

In a saucepan bring 1.5 litres of water to the boil and blanch the livers, then remove and cut into thin slices. Add the giblets, garlic, peppercorns and half the ginger to the pan and cook for 10 minutes, then strain through a fine sieve.

Heat the oil in a clean pan and sauté the remaining ginger for 3 minutes, then add the chicken liver and mushroom and cook for a further minute.

Pour in the stock and bring to the boil, then add the wine and soy sauce. Allow to simmer for 10 minutes, then transfer to a soup tureen. Heat the sesame oil and sprinkle over the soup. Garnish with fresh basil leaves.

SOP KAMPING (lamb soup) — *Malaysia*

400 g fresh lamb chops
2 Tbsp vegetable oil
1 small onion, finely chopped
1 tsp finely chopped garlic
1 Tbsp finely chopped fresh ginger
150 g fresh beancurd,
  cut into small cubes
2 fresh red chillies, finely chopped
salt & pepper to taste
1 Tbsp fresh lime juice
1 Tbsp crispy-fried shallot
2 tsp freshly chopped coriander

Trim any excess fat from the meat, then chop into small bite-size chunks.

Heat the oil in a large pan and stir-fry the lamb for 2-3 minutes to seal in the flavour, then remove and drain on kitchen paper. Add the onion, garlic and ginger and sauté for 2 minutes, then replace the meat, add the beancurd and chillies and season to taste with salt and pepper.

Pour in 1.5 litres of cold water and bring to the boil, then cover the pan, lower heat and allow to simmer until the meat is tender, approximately 1 hour. Finally, stir in the lime juice and simmer for a further minute, then transfer to a soup tureen. Garnish with crispy-fried shallot and freshly chopped coriander.

SOP LEMBU (oxtail soup) — *Malaysia*

850 g oxtail
salt & freshly ground black pepper
2 Tbsp plain flour
2 onions, chopped
2 carrots, sliced
1 stick celery, chopped

1 leek, sliced
2 Tbsp butter
1.5 litres beef stock
2 tsp fresh lemon juice
2 Tbsp crispy fried shallot

Wash and joint the oxtail. Dry thoroughly, then season with salt and pepper and dust lightly with flour.

Heat the butter in a large pan and sauté the onion for 3-4 minutes, then add the carrot, celery, leek and oxtail and cook for a further 3 minutes.

Add the stock, cover and cook over a low heat until the meat is tender, then strain into a clean pan. Remove meat from the bones and cut into small dice.

Bring the stock back to the boil, add the meat and lemon juice and adjust seasonings to taste. Stir and cook for a further 2 minutes, then transfer to a soup tureen and sprinkle the crispy fried shallot on top.

PHO BAHN (beef noodle soup) — *Vietnam*

3 kilos meaty beef bones
2 Tbsp vegetable oil
2 large brown onion, sliced
3 cm knob fresh ginger, sliced
4 cloves
4 star anise
10 cm stick cinnamon
2 bay leaves

1 Tbsp fish sauce
1 tsp freshly ground black pepper
450 g rump steak,
  cut into paper-thin slices
4 spring onions, finely sliced
400 g rice noodles
1 Tbsp hot chilli sauce

Place the bones in a pot and cover with cold water. Bring to the boil and cook for 10 minutes, then drain and rinse the pot. Replace the bones, cover with 2.5 litres of water and bring back to the boil.

Heat the oil and sauté the onion and ginger for 5 minutes, then transfer to the pot. Add the cloves, star anise, cinnamon stick and bay leaves and season with fish sauce and pepper. Cover the pot and allow to simmer for 2 hours, then remove the cover and retain over a moderate heat for a further 30-40 minutes. Strain the stock into a fresh pan and add the chilli sauce.

Meanwhile, soak the noodles in cold water for 20 minutes, then drain in a colander and plunge into a pan of rapidly boiling water. Immediately remove pan from heat and allow to stand for 3 minutes, then again drain the noodles.

Arrange the noodles in individual soup bowls, top with paper thin slices of beef and finely shredded spring onion and add boiling stock.

MIANG PLA TOO (spicy mackerel salad) — *Thailand*

4 small mackerel
100 ml vegetable oil
75 g roasted peanuts, shelled
4 shallots, finely sliced
2 tsp finely chopped ginger
1 tsp finely chopped garlic
4 fresh red chillies, finely sliced
4 fresh green chillies, finely sliced

75 g shredded green mango
1 tsp shredded lime peel
2 Tbsp fresh lime juice
1 Tbsp fish sauce
2 tsp sugar
0.5 tsp freshly ground black pepper
lettuce leaves
fresh mint leaves

Prepare the fish and steam until partially cooked. Heat the oil in a shallow pan and fry the fish for 4-5 minutes, turning once. Remove the skin and carefully discard all the bones, then flake the meat and place in a bowl.

Add the shallot, ginger, garlic, chilli, mango, lime peel, lime juice, fish sauce, sugar and pepper and toss to combine thoroughly. Chill for 30 minutes.

Arrange lettuce leaves in a bowl, add the salad and garnish with mint leaves.

GOI SUA TOM THIT (jellyfish salad)   *Vietnam*

150 g jellyfish
75 g boiled shrimps
2 Tbsp sugar
75 ml vinegar
1 Tbsp fish sauce
100 g shredded carrot
1 Tbsp shredded radish
1 Tbsp finely chopped onion
1 Tbsp finely chopped celery
1 Tbsp chopped coriander leaves
1 Tbsp chopped mint leaves
75 g roasted pork, thinly sliced
freshly ground black pepper
1 Tbsp chopped peanuts

Soak the jellyfish in cold water for 10 minutes, then pat dry and shred finely. Shell and de-vein the shrimps and cut in half lengthways. Dissolve half the sugar with vinegar and the remainder with fish sauce.

In a salad bowl, combine the carrot and radish with the vinegar, then add the onion, celery, coriander, mint, pork, shrimps and jellyfish.

Season with pepper and toss to combine thoroughly, then chill for 30 minutes. Garnish with chopped peanuts just before serving.

KINALAW NA TANGUIGUE (mackerel with coconut dressing)   *Philippines*

500 g mackerel fillets
250 ml vinegar
250 g grated coconut
6 shallots, finely sliced
2 Tbsp finely chopped ginger

2 fresh green chillies, finely sliced
2 tsp sea salt
0.5 tsp freshly ground black pepper
raw onion rings

Remove any skin from the fish fillets. Chop the flesh into small bite-size cubes and wash in half the vinegar.

In a non-reactive bowl combine the grated coconut with the remaining vinegar and strain the liquid into a glass mixing bowl. Add the fish, shallot, ginger, chilli, salt and pepper and stir to blend thoroughly.

Chill in the refrigerator for 30 minutes, then transfer to a serving platter and garnish with onion rings.

GADO GADO (mixed salad with peanut dressing) *Indonesia*

2 potatoes
125 g white cabbage, shredded
125 g spinach leaves, chopped
125 g green bean, sliced
100 g bean sprouts, trimmed
50 ml peanut oil
150 g beancurd, sliced
100 g cucumber. sliced
3 hard boiled eggs, quartered
8 shrimp crackers

Sauce:
2 shallots, chopped
3 fresh red chillies, chopped
1 tsp chopped garlic
2 tsp crumbled shrimp paste
2 Tbsp peanut oil
150 g roasted peanuts, ground
1 Tbsp sugar
1 Tbsp dark soy sauce
2 Tbsp tamarind water

Boil the potatoes, allow to cool, then slice. Boil the cabbage, spinach, beans and beansprouts separately until each is barely tender. Do not overcook. Heat the oil and fry the slices of beancurd until golden, then remove and drain.

Pound the shallot, chilli, garlic and shrimp paste with 1 tsp oil to produce a smooth paste. Heat the remaining oil in a saucepan and stir-fry the spice paste for 4-5 minutes, then add the sugar, soy sauce and 200 ml water. Bring to the boil, then stir in the ground peanuts and cook over a moderate heat, stirring occasionally, until the sauce thickens.Finally, add the tamarind water, adjust seasonings to taste and stir for a further minute, then set aside to cool.

Arrange the vegetables and beancurd on a platter and surround with cucumber and hard-boiled eggs. Pour on the sauce and serve with prawn crackers.

THANATSONE (broccoli salad) *Myanmar*

600 g broccoli
2 onions, finely sliced
4 cloves garlic, finely sliced
150 ml vegetable oil
2 Tbsp sesame oil

0.5 tsp ground turmeric
50 ml white vinegar
salt to taste
freshly ground black pepper
2 Tbsp toasted sesame seeds

Cut the broccoli into bite-size pieces and cook in rapidly boiling water until barely tender, approximately 2 minutes, then drain in a colander and pat dry.

Combine the vegetable and sesame oils in a saucepan and set over a high heat. When the oil is very hot, add the onion and garlic and cook until the onion starts to brown, then remove pan from heat and stir continuously for 2-3 minutes. Set aside for oil to cool, then add broccoli, vinegar, salt and pepper and toss well.

Remove the broccoli from the oil and drain on kitchen paper, then transfer to a salad bowl and sprinkle the sesame seeds on top.

GADO GADO (mixed salad with peanut dressing)

SOM TUM (green papaya salad)   *Thailand*

200 g green papaya, shredded
12 tsp grated ginger
1 tsp minced garlic
1 tsp finely chopped red chilli
1 tsp finely chopped green chilli
75 g green beans, sliced
75 g shredded cabbage
75 g shredded carrot
4 cherry tomatoes, halved
75 g fresh lime juice
2 Tbsp fish sauce
2 Tbsp sugar
1 Tbsp ground dried shrimp
1 Tbsp ground peanuts

In a mortar, pound together the papaya, ginger and garlic until smooth, then transfer to a bowl and add the chilli, beans, cabbage, carrot and tomato.

Combine lime juice, fish sauce and sugar and stir until the sugar has dissolved. Pour half the dressing over the salad and toss well, then sprinkle the ground dried shrimp and ground peanuts on top and add the remaining dressing.

Chill for at least 1 hour before serving.

SUNOMONO (vegetable salad)   *Japan*

200 g shredded cabbage
100 g shredded carrot
100 g finely sliced cucumber
2 Tbsp shredded radish
75 ml vinegar
2 Tbsp sweet soy sauce

2 Tbsp rice wine
1 Tbsp fresh lemon juice
1 Tbsp sugar
1 Tbsp dried fish flakes
2 egg yolks
salt & black pepper to taste

Arrange the vegetables in a salad bowl.

In a saucepan, bring the vinegar, soy sauce, wine and lemon juice to the boil, then add the sugar and fish flakes and stir until the sugar has dissolved. Lower heat and allow to simmer for 5 minutes, then strain into a fresh pan.

Bring back to a low boil, then add the egg yolk and season to taste. Stir until the sauce thickens slightly, then remove from heat and allow to cool.

Pour the sauce over the vegetables and toss lightly, then chill before serving.

YAAM NUEA (spicy beef salad)   *Thailand*

450 g beef fillet
2 shallots, finely chopped
1 tsp finely chopped garlic
2 tsp finely chopped coriander
2 Tbsp sugar
0.5 tsp salt
0.5 tsp freshly ground black pepper

1 Tbsp light soy sauce
2 tsp fresh lime juice
2 Tbsp vegetable oil
6 fresh green chillies, finely sliced
lettuce leaves
1.5 Tbsp finely sliced spring onion
fresh coriander leaves

Cook the beef to medium rare and cut into thin slices. Pound together the shallot, garlic, ginger, coriander, sugar, salt, pepper, soy sauce and lime juice to produce a smooth paste.

Heat the oil in a frying pan and stir-fry the spice paste for 3-4 minutes, then add the beef and cook for a further minute. Remove beef and set aside to cool, then add the chilli and mix well.

Arrange lettuce leaves in a salad bowl and add the beef, then sprinkle the spring onion on top and garnish with fresh coriander leaves.

Seafood

TEMPURA (deep-fried seafood with vegetables), *recipe page 74)*

SAMBAL UDANG (prawns in coconut sauce) — *Malaysia*

500 g fresh prawns
4 dried chillies, soaked and chopped
4 shallots, chopped
1 Tbsp finely chopped ginger
2 candlenuts, chopped
2 tsp chopped garlic
1 tsp ground coriander
1 tsp ground turmeric

3 Tbsp vegetable oil
1.5 Tbsp fresh lime juice
2 tomatoes, skinned and chopped
1 Tbsp palm sugar
salt to taste
freshly ground black pepper
300 ml thick coconut milk
freshly chopped coriander leaves

Shell and de-vein the prawns, leaving the tails attached.

Pound together the chilli, shallot, ginger, candlenut, garlic, coriander, turmeric and 1 tsp oil to produce a smooth paste. Heat the remaining oil in a wok and stir-fry the spice paste for 4-5 minutes, then add 150 ml water and the lime juice and bring to the boil.

Add the tomato, sugar, salt and propping requiredepper, then lower heat and allow to simmer for 3-4 minutes. Add the coconut milk, bring back to the boil and stir until the sauce starts to thicken, then add the prawns.

Cook over a moderate heat, for 2-3 minutes, stirring occasionally, until the prawns are tender, then transfer to a serving dish and garnish with coriander.

HAR KOU CHOI SUM (fried prawns with greens) *Hong Kong*

8 fresh king prawns
1 egg white
2 tsp cornflour
1 tsp sugar
0.5 tsp salt
0.5 tsp white pepper
3 Tbsp vegetable oil
300 g choi sum
2 Tbsp chicken stock
2 tsp Chinese wine
1 tsp oyster sauce
2 tsp finely chopped ham

Shell and de-vein the prawns and place in a shallow dish. Beat the egg-white lightly with the cornflour, sugar, salt and pepper and pour over the prawns. Stir to coat evenly, then set aside for 30 minutes.

Heat half the oil in a wok until it starts to smoke, then lower heat to moderate and add the choi sum and a pinch of salt. Stir-fry for 2 minutes, then remove and drain on kitchen paper. Add remaining oil to the wok and stir-fry the prawns over a high heat for 30 seconds, then remove and drain.

Add the stock, wine and oyster sauce and stir to combine, then replace the choi sum and prawns and adjust seasonings to taste. Cook for a further minute, then transfer to a serving dish and garnish with finely chopped ham.

CHINGRI MALAI (prawn coconut curry) *India*

650 g fresh prawns
1 tsp ground turmeric
0.5 tsp salt
2 Tbsp finely chopped onions
1 Tbsp finely chopped ginger

1 Tbsp finely chopped garlic
1 Tbsp finely chopped green chilli
75 ml olive oil
300 ml thick coconut milk

Shell and de-vein the prawns and rub with turmeric and salt, then set aside for 15 minutes. Pound together the onion, ginger, garlic and chilli to produce a paste.

Heat oil in a pan and sauté the prawns for 2 minutes, then remove with a slotted spoon and set aside.

Reheat the oil, add the spice paste and stir-fry for 2 minutes, then add the coconut milk and bring to the boil. Simmer until the sauce has reduced by half, then add the prawns, adjust seasonings to taste and stir for a further minute.

SUEN TIM HAR (sweet & sour prawns) *Hong Kong*

675 g fresh prawns
1 egg, lightly beaten
3 Tbsp vinegar
1 Tbsp Chinese wine
1 Tbsp light soy sauce
2 tsp sugar
0.5 tsp freshly ground black

3 Tbsp cornflour
75 ml vegetable oil
1 large onion, chopped
2 tsp chopped ginger
1 green pepper, chopped
3 fresh red chillies, sliced
150 g can pineapple chunks

Shell and de-vein the prawns and place in a shallow dish, then season with salt and pepper. Combine the egg, vinegar, wine, soy sauce and sugar and pour over the prawns. Stir to coat the prawns evenly, then set aside for 30 minutes. Remove prawns and dust with cornflour. Retain the marinade.

Heat half the oil in a wok and sauté the prawns for 2 minutes, then remove and drain on kitchen paper. Wipe wok clean, add remaining oil and reheat.

Add the onion, ginger, pepper and chilli and stir-fry for 4-5 minutes, then add the spring onion, remaining vinegar and reserved marinade. Bring to the boil, add the prawns, and pineapple chunks and stir for 2 minutes, then transfer to a warm dish and serve immediately.

JIANG JIAO DA XIA (chilli prawns with ginger) *Singapore*

600 g fresh prawns
salt and pepper
1 egg white
2 tsp cornflour
3 Tbsp Chinese wine
oil for deep frying
6 fresh red chillies, finely sliced
1 Tbsp finely chopped ginger

2 tsp crushed garlic
1 Tbsp sugar
1 Tbsp light soy sauce
1 tsp dark soy sauce
1 tsp rice vinegar
1 Tbsp finely chopped spring onion
1 Tbsp freshly chopped coriander

Shell and de-vein the prawns and place in a shallow dish, then season with salt and pepper. Beat the egg with the cornflour and half the wine and pour over the prawns. Set aside for 20 minutes, turning once.

Heat the oil in a wok until it starts to smoke, then lower heat slightly and fry the prawns until golden and crispy. Remove and drain on kitchen paper. Pour off most of the oil and reheat the wok.

Add the chilli, ginger and garlic and stir-fry over a moderately hot heat for 3 minutes, then add soy sauce, vinegar, sugar and remaining wine and bring to the boil. Lower heat, then add the prawns and spring onion.

Stir and cook for a further minute, then transfer to a serving dish and garnish with freshly chopped coriander.

GOONG PAD (prawns with chilli paste) — *Thailand*

500 g fresh prawns
1 shallot, finely chopped
2 fresh red chillies, finely chopped
2.5 cm knob ginger, finely chopped
2 tsp finely chopped lemon grass
1 tsp finely chopped garlic
0.25 tsp grated nutmeg
1 tsp chopped shrimp paste
0.5 tsp salt
0.5 tsp freshly ground black pepper
1 Tbsp fresh lime juice
250 ml thick coconut milk
150 g rice flour
oil for deep frying

Shell and de-vein the prawns and place in a bowl. Place all the dry ingredients, apart from the rice flour, in a bowl, add the lime juice and coconut milk and mix thoroughly, then pour over the prawns.

Stir to ensure the prawns are coated evenly and set aside for 30 minutes. Then remove and dust with rice flour.

Heat the oil in a wok until it starts to smoke, then lower heat slightly and deep-fry the prawns for 1-2 minutes, then remove with a slotted spoon and drain on kitchen paper. Serve immediately.

ZHENG DA XIA (steamed prawns) — *China*

650 g large fresh prawns
2.5 cm knob fresh ginger
2 Tbsp Chinese wine
2 tsp sesame oil
0.25 tsp five-spice powder

0.5 tsp salt
0.25 tsp freshly ground white pepper
2 tsp chilli oil
2 Tbsp finely chopped spring onion.

Shell and de-vein the prawns, cut in half lengthways, and arrange in a shallow heatproof dish. Julienne the ginger and place over the prawns, then sprinkle with wine and sesame oil and season with five-spice powder, salt and pepper.

Place the dish on a rack and set in a wok containing a little water. Bring to the boil, cover the wok with a tightly-fitting lid and steam for 5-6 minutes.

Remove the dish, sprinkle chilli oil over the prawns and garnish with finely chopped spring onion. Serve immediately.

TOM BO NUONG LUI (prawn rolls)   *Vietnam*

8 king prawns
250 g minced beef
2 tsp finely chopped lemon grass
1 tsp minced garlic
1 tsp oyster sauce
1 tsp sesame oil
1 tsp sugar
0.5 tsp salt
0.5 tsp freshly ground black pepper
8 paper thin slices beef
4 rashers streaky bacon, halved

Shell and de-vein the prawns, leaving the tails attached.

Place the minced beef in a bowl together with the lemon grass, garlic, oyster sauce, sesame oil, sugar, salt and pepper and combine thoroughly.

Lay the slices of beef on a flat surface and place a prawn on each, then top with a little stuffing. Roll the beef around the prawn, then wrap with the bacon and secure with toothpicks.

Cook over charcoal or under a hot grill for 10-12 minutes, then transfer to a platter and serve with a garlic-chilli dip.

PRATAAD LOM (prawn crepes)   *Thailand*

12 medium size prawns
2 tsp chopped coriander root
1 tsp finely chopped garlic
1 tsp finely chopped lemon grass

10 black peppercorns
3 Tbsp fish sauce
12 soy bean crepes
vegetable oil for deep frying

Shell and de-vein the prawns. Pound together the coriander root, lemon grass, and garlic until smooth, then add the fish sauce and stir to combine.

Add the prawns and set aside for 10 minutes, turning at least once to ensure an even coating of marinade. Then, wrap each prawn in a crepe and moisten the edges with a little water to seal.

Heat the oil in a wok until it starts to smoke, then lower heat slightly, add the prawn crepes and cook until golden. Remove with a slotted spoon and drain on kitchen paper, then transfer to a platter and serve with a sweet chilli sauce.

GOAN BORO ESSA KORI (curried lobster) *India*

2 live lobsters, approx. 650 g each
2 Tbsp dried tamarind
150 g freshly grated coconut
6 dried red chillies
1 Tbsp coriander seeds
1 Tbsp cumin seeds
8 black peppercorns

1 tsp ground turmeric
3 Tbsp vegetable oil
2 tomatoes, chopped
2 onions, chopped
25 mm knob fresh ginger, chopped
4 fresh green chillies, finely sliced
salt to taste

Bring a large pan of water to a rapid boil and add lobsters. Cover with a tightly fitting lid and cook for 8-10 minutes, until lobsters turn a bright pink. Remove the lobsters and allow to cool. Break off claws and tails, carefully remove all the meat and cut into chunks.

Soak the tamarind in 100 ml cold water for 30 minutes, then squeeze and reserve the pulp. Grind together the coconut, dried chillies, coriander, cumin, peppercorns and turmeric, then mix with 100 ml cold water to produce a smooth paste.

Heat the oil in a pan, add the tomato, onion, ginger and green chilli and sauté for 5 minutes, then add coconut paste and continue to cook, stirring frequently, for a further 7-8 minutes.

Add the lobster to the pan and season to taste with salt. Allow to simmer for 2-3 minutes, then stir in the tamarind pulp and cook for a final 2 minutes.

ZIANG LONG XIA (stir-fried lobster)   *Singapore*

2 fresh lobsters, approx. 600 g each
salt and pepper
2 tsp cornflour
100 ml peanut oil
2 tsp finely chopped ginger
1 tsp finely chopped garlic

2 spring onions, finely chopped
2 Tbsp Chinese wine
2 tsp light soy sauce
200 ml clear fish stock
sprig of fresh coriander

Boil the lobsters and allow to cool. Break off the tails, crack the claws and carefully remove all the meat. Cut the meat into small chunks, season with salt and pepper and dust with cornflour. Set aside for 20 minutes.

Heat the oil in a wok and stir-fry the lobster for 1 minute, then remove and drain on kitchen paper. Pour away most of the oil and re-heat the wok. Add the ginger and garlic and stir-fry for 3 minutes, then add the spring onion and cook for a further minute.

Replace the lobster, add the wine, soy sauce, sugar and stock and bring to the boil. Lower heat, adjust seasonings to taste and allow to simmer for 1 minute, then transfer to a warm serving plate and garnish with fresh coriander.

LUNG HAI CHAU DAN (lobster omelette)   *Hong Kong*

350 g cooked lobster meat
salt and pepper
3 Tbsp peanut oil
3 cm knob ginger, finely chopped
1 tsp minced garlic
2 spring onions, finely chopped

2 Tbsp chopped green pepper
1.5 Tbsp Chinese wine
1 Tbsp light soy sauce
8 fresh eggs, lightly beaten
1 tsp sesame oil
1 tsp freshly chopped coriander

Chop the lobster into small chunks and season with salt and pepper.

Heat 1 Tbsp oil in a wok and stir-fry the ginger and garlic for 3 minutes, then add the lobster, spring onion, pepper, wine and soy sauce, stir well and bring to the boil.

Lower heat, adjust seasonings to taste and cook for 2 minutes, then transfer to a mixing bowl. Allow to cool slightly, then add the beaten egg and sesame oil and stir to mix well.

Heat the remaining oil in a clean wok and pour in the mixture. Cook over a low to moderate heat until the egg sets, turning once and breaking up slightly. Transfer to a warm plate and serve immediately.

ZIANG LONG XIA (stir-fried lobster)

KAKEDA KARI (crab curry) — *India*

4 crabs, approx 300 g each
4 onions, chopped
100 ml vegetable oil
12 dried red chillies
8 cloves
4 cardamom seeds
1 Tbsp coriander seeds
0.5 tsp cumin seeds

8 cm cinnamon stick
1 Tbsp black peppercorns
3 Tbsp tamarind pulp
2 Tbsp grated coconut
0.5 tsp ground turmeric
75 ml thick coconut milk
salt to taste
freshly chopped coriander leaves

Chop the crabs into bite-size pieces.

Heat 2 Tbsp oil in a pan and fry half the onion until brown, then remove and drain on kitchen paper. Add the chillies, cloves, cardamoms, coriander seeds, cumin seeds, cinnamon and peppercorns to the pan and stir for 2-3 minutes, then transfer to a mortar, add the tamarind and fried onion and pound to produce a smooth paste.

Heat a further 2 Tbsp oil in a clean pan and stir-fry the coconut and turmeric for 2-3 minutes, then pound this to a smooth paste. Add the remaining oil to the pan and stir-fry the remaining onion for 2 minutes, then add the crab and cook for 6 minutes, stirring frequently. Add the spice and coconut pastes and stir well, then add 75 ml water and bring to the boil.

Lower heat and allow to simmer for 5 minutes, then add the coconut milk and bring back to the boil. Lower heat, add salt to taste, and cook over a moderate heat until the sauce starts to thicken, then transfer to a serving dish and garnish with freshly chopped coriander.

CUA RAM MUOI (salt & pepper crabs) — *Vietnam*

8 fresh blue crabs
50 ml peanut oil
1 Tbsp finely chopped shallot
2 tsp finely chopped garlic

1 Tbsp Chinese wine
1 tsp salt
0.5 tsp freshly ground black pepper

Cook the crabs until they turn bright red. Allow to cool, then break off the claws and cut the bodies into large bite-size pieces. Smash the shells lightly with a kitchen mallet to make the meat easier to extract

Heat the oil in a wok until it starts to smoke and sauté the shallot and garlic for 3-4 minutes, then add the crab and cover the wok. Cook for 6-8 minutes, tossing frequently, then uncover, add the wine and cook for a further minute.

Sprinkle with salt and pepper and toss well, then transfer to a warm platter and serve immediately.

CHI ZHI XIE (crab in black bean sauce) *China*

2 large crabs
1 egg white, lightly beaten with
  2 tsp dark soy sauce
  0.5 tsp white pepper
  2 tsp cornflour
1 Tbsp fermented black beans
2 Tbsp peanut oil
50 ml vegetable oil
1 onion, finely chopped

1 green pepper, chopped
1 Tbsp finely chopped ginger
2 tsp minced garlic
1 tsp sugar
1 Tbsp Chinese wine
1 Tbsp light soy sauce
1 tsp sesame oil
125 ml chicken stock
2 tsp cornflour

Boil the crab, then allow to cool, extract all the meat and place in a bowl. Mash the fermented beans with the peanut oil to produce a smooth paste.

Heat the vegetable oil in a wok until it starts to smoke, then lower heat slightly and stir-fry crab meat for 1 minute. Add the onion and green pepper and cook for a further 2 minutes, then remove with a slotted spoon and drain.

Pour away most of the oil and re-heat the wok. Add the ginger and garlic and stir-fry for 2 minutes, then add the fermented bean paste and continue to stir for a further minute.

Add the sugar, wine, soy sauce, sesame oil and stock and bring to the boil, then replace the crab and vegetables, stir-well and adjust seasonings to taste.

Finally, mix the cornflour with a little cold water and stir into the sauce to thicken slightly, then transfer to a warm plate and serve immediately.

ALIMASAG AT LANGA SA GATA
(coconut crab with jackfruit)

Philippines

3 crabs, approx. 350 g each
500 ml thick coconut milk
300 g jackfruit flesh, flaked
1 small onion, sliced
3 cm knob ginger, julienne
2 tsp minced garlic

6 stems lemon grass,
*   white parts only, sliced*
sea salt to taste
freshly ground black pepper
500 ml coconut cream
75 g green chillies

Clean the crabs and cut into quarters.

Place the coconut milk, jackfruit, onion, ginger, garlic and lemon grass in a casserole and boil over a moderate heat for 10 minutes, then add the crabs and season to taste with salt and pepper. Reduce heat, cover the casserole and allow to simmer for 15-20 minutes.

Meanwhile, in a saucepan, bring the coconut cream to the boil and cook, stirring continuously, until the cream is thick enough to coat the ladle, then add to the crab. Stir well, then add the chillies and simmer for a further 5 minutes. Serve immediately.

KEPITING PEDAS (spicy crab claws) — *Indonesia*

12 crab claws
3 Tbsp vegetable oil
3 shallots, finely chopped
2 tsp finely chopped ginger
1 tsp finely chopped garlic
2 tsp finely chopped fresh red chilli
1 tsp finely chopped lemon grass
0.5 tsp ground coriander
0.5 tsp ground cumin
0.5 tsp ground turmeric
salt to taste
freshly ground black pepper
2 tsp fresh lime juice

Boil the crab claws until they turn bright red, then drain and set aside.

Heat the oil in a pan and sauté the shallot, ginger and garlic for 2 minutes, then add the chilli, lemon grass and ground spices and stir for a further 2 minutes.

Add the coconut milk and bring to the boil, then add the crab claws and season with salt and pepper. Lower heat and allow to simmer for 3-4 minutes, then transfer to a serving dish and sprinkle with lime juice.

KAKULWO (curried coconut crab) — *Sri Lanka*

2 large crabs
4 shallots, chopped
6 green chillies, finely chopped
1 Tbsp finely chopped ginger
2 tsp minced garlic
6 curry leaves
0.5 tsp ground turmeric
0.5 tsp ground fenugreek

8 cm cinnamon stick
750 ml thin coconut milk
300 ml thick coconut milk
2 Tbsp grated coconut
1 Tbsp ground rice
2 Tbsp fresh lime juice
salt to taste
fresh coriander leaves.

Place the crabs in a pan of rapidly boiling water for 5 minutes, then remove the claws and smash slightly and chop the body into bite-size pieces.

Place the crab in a deep pan, add the shallot, chillies, ginger, garlic, curry leaves, turmeric, fenugreek, cinnamon and the thin coconut milk and bring to the boil. Cover the pan and simmer over a moderate heat for 6-8 minutes.

Combine the grated coconut, rice, salt, lime juice and thick coconut milk and add to the pan. Bring back to the boil, then lower heat and allow to simmer over a low heat for 10 minutes, then transfer to a dish and garnish with fresh coriander.

PO TAEK (sour seafood pot)   *Thailand*

8 mussels
2 crab claws
6 fresh prawns
200 g sea bass fillets
250 g fresh squid
1.25 litres clear fish stock

2 pickled plums
2 Tbsp fish sauce
freshly ground black pepper
3 cm knob fresh ginger, chopped
4 fresh red chillies, finely sliced
2 Tbsp fresh lime juice

Scrub the mussels with a wire brush and rinse in salted water, then cook in a steamer, discarding any that fail to open.

Crack the crab claws, remove the meat and cut into chunks. Shell and de-vein the prawns, leaving tails attached. Cut the sea bass into bite-size pieces. Discard the head and ink sac from the squid, then cut into bite size pieces.

Pour the stock into a large clay pot and bring to the boil, then add picked plums, fish sauce and pepper. Lower heat and allow to simmer for 10 minutes, then add the ginger, chilli, lime juice and seafoods.

Retain over a moderate heat, stirring occasionally, until the seafood is cooked, then transfer to a serving dish and garnish with fresh coriander leaves.

HAW MOG HOY (spicy steamed mussels)   *Thailand*

1 kilo mussels
2 Tbsp vegetable oil
2 shallots, chopped
2 tsp finely chopped garlic
2 tsp finely chopped ginger
4 fresh red chillies, finely sliced
1 tsp chopped coriander root

1 tsp chopped lemon grass
1 tsp chopped lime peel
2 tsp crumbled shrimp paste
1 egg, lightly beaten
175 ml coconut cream
2 Tbsp rice flour
sweet basil leaves

Prepare and steam mussels (see above). Retain larger shells in warming oven.

Heat the oil in a pan and sauté the shallot and garlic for 3 minutes, then add the ginger, chilli, coriander, lemon grass, lime peel and shrimp paste.

Stir and cook over a moderate heat until the mixture gives off a fragrant aroma, then transfer to a mixing bowl, add the egg, coconut cream and flour. Season to taste and stir to blend thoroughly.

Blanch the basil leaves and arrange in the retained shells. Add 2 mussels to each shell and spoon a little sauce on top and arrange on an ovenproof plate.

Place in a steamer and cook over rapidly boiling water until the mussels are heated through, then serve immediately.

HOY MALAENG POO LAAM — *Thailand*

675 g mussels
125 g cooked crabmeat
125 g white fish fillets,
   steamed and finely chopped
1 tsp shredded lime leaves
1 tsp shredded balsam leaves
2 Tbsp hot chilli paste

2 Tbsp palm sugar
6 eggs, lightly whisked
2 Tbsp fish sauce
0.5 tsp freshly ground black pepper
175 ml coconut cream
bamboo tubes (see below)

Scrub the mussels with a stiff wire brush and wash in salted water. Cook in rapidly boiling water until they all open, discarding any that fail to do so, then remove from the shell.

Pass the mussels and crabmeat through a coarse grinder and place in a mixing bowl with the fish, leaves, chilli paste, egg, fish sauce, sugar, pepper and all but 2 Tbsp of the coconut cream. Stir to combine thoroughly.

Transfer the mixture to the bamboo tubes and top with the remaining coconut cream. Cover with kitchen foil and place under a moderately hot grill for 15 minutes, then remove and continue to cook until the mixture is set and the top is golden.

The appropriate bamboo tubes should be approximately 10 cm in diameter, halved, and cut in to lengths of 20 cm. Before using, scrub clean in salted water and dry thoroughly.

XIANG LA CHAO XIAN (spicy fried cockles) *Singapore*

650 g cockles
3 Tbsp peanut oil
2 shallots, finely chopped
4 fresh red chillies, finely chopped
2 tsp finely chopped ginger
2 tsp crushed garlic
1 Tbsp sweet chilli sauce
1 Tbsp black bean sauce
2 tsp dark soy sauce
salt to taste
freshly ground black pepper
2 tsp cornflour
2 tsp fresh lime juice

Place the cockles in boiling water for 2 minutes, then remove from the shells.

Heat the oil in a wok until very hot, then add the shallot, chilli, ginger and garlic and stir-fry for 3 minutes. Add the sweet chilli sauce, black bean sauce, soy sauce and 125 ml cold water and bring to the boil, then season to taste with salt and pepper. Lower heat and allow to simmer for 3-4 minutes.

Finally, mix the cornflour with a small quantity of cold water and stir into the sauce to thicken slightly, then transfer to a serving dish and sprinkle the fresh lime juice on top.

TAHONG ADOBO (clams in vinegar-garlic sauce) *Philippines*

1 kilo littleneck, or razor, clams
2 Tbsp vegetable oil
1 Tbsp finely chopped onion
1 Tbsp finely chopped garlic

2 tsp finely chopped ginger
100 ml vinegar
0.5 crushed black peppercorns
0.5 tsp sea salt

Steam the clams until they all open, discarding any that fail to do so.

Heat the oil in a pan and sauté the onion, garlic and ginger for 2-3 minutes, then add the vinegar and bring to the boil.

Add the clams, season to taste with salt and pepper and allow to simmer over a moderate heat for 5 minutes, then transfer to a dish and serve immediately.

JU YIM SIN YAU (squid with chilli and garlic)   *Hong Kong*

450 g medium size squid
1 tsp salt
0.5 tsp freshly ground white pepper
1 Tbsp fresh lime juice
75 ml vegetable oil
1 Tbsp finely chopped onion
2 tsp finely chopped ginger

2 tsp finely chopped garlic
8 fresh red chillies, finely chopped
1 Tbsp Chinese wine
2 tsp dark soy sauce
1 tsp sugar
1 Tbsp finely chopped spring onion

Clean the squid and discard ink sacs and heads. Cut the squid down the centre and, with a sharp knife, make shallow criss-cross incisions in the flesh. Place squid in a dish and season with salt and pepper, then sprinkle with lime juice. Set aside for 30 minutes, then cut into bit-size pieces.

Heat the oil in a wok and sauté the onion, ginger and garlic for 3 minutes, then add the chilli and stir for a further minute.

Add the squid and stir-fry over a fairly high heat for 2 minutes, then add the wine, soy sauce and sugar and adjust seasonings to taste. Continue to cook for a further 2-3 minutes, then remove and drain on kitchen paper.

Transfer to a warm serving dish and garnish with the chopped spring onion

PLA MUEG PAAD PRIG (squid in hot sauce)   *Thailand*

450 g squid, cleaned and prepared
3 Tbsp vegetable oil
2 shallots, finely chopped
2 tsp finely chopped garlic
1 Tbsp finely chopped red chilli
1 Tbsp chopped spring onion

2 tsp fish sauce
2 tsp oyster sauce
1 Tbsp rice wine
0.5 tsp freshly ground black pepper
1 Tbsp freshly chopped coriander

Cut the squid into bite-size pieces and parboil for 2-3 minutes, then pour into a colander and set aside.

Heat the oil in a pan and saute the shallot and garlic until golden, then add the squid, chilli and spring onion. Stir for a further minute, then add the fish sauce, oyster sauce, wine, stock and pepper and bring to the boil.

Cook over a moderate heat, stirring occasionally, until the squid is tender, then add the coriander and mix well.

Stir for a further minute, then transfer to a dish and serve immediately.

CUMI CUMI ISI (stuffed squid)   *Indonesia*

500 g medium-size squid
2 tsp coarse salt
2 Tbsp fresh lime juice
2 shallots, finely chopped
2 tsp finely chopped fresh red chilli
2 tsp finely chopped ginger
1 tsp minced garlic
1 tsp finely chopped lemon grass

2 candlenuts, finely chopped
150 g finely chopped chicken breast
0.5 tsp salt
0.5 tsp freshly ground black pepper
3 Tbsp vegetable oil
250 ml thin coconut milk
2 tsp finely sliced spring onion

Clean the squid and discard the ink sacs and heads. Remove tentacles and chop finely. Rub the salt over the squid and place in a shallow dish, then add the lime juice and set aside for 15 minutes, turning occasionally.

Combine the shallot, chilli, ginger, garlic, lemon grass, candlenut, chicken meat and chopped tentacles and season with salt and pepper. Stuff mixture inside the squid and secure ends with toothpicks.

Heat the oil in a wok and sauté the squid for 3-4 minutes, then remove and drain on kitchen paper.

Pour away the remaining oil from the wok, then add the coconut milk and bring to the boil. Add the squid, then lower heat, cover the pan and allow to simmer until the squid is tender, approximately 5 minutes.

Remove squid with a slotted spoon and transfer to a serving dish. Bring stock to a rapid boil and reduce by half, then pour over the squid and garnish with spring onion. Serve immediately.

TEMPURA (deep-fried seafood with vegetables) *Japan*

12 large prawns
400 g fish fillets
8 shitake mushrooms
2 brown onions
4 spring onions
1 small aubergine
4 asparagus spears
225 g can bamboo shoots, drained
16 gingko nuts
oil for deep frying

Batter:
2 fresh eggs
200 g plain flour
0.25 tsp baking soda
Sauce:
75 ml mirin (sweet rice wine)
75 ml shoyu (Japanese soy sauce)
125 ml dashi (see below)
0.25 tsp salt
2 Tbsp finely grated white radish

Shell and de-vein the prawns leaving the tails intact. Remove any skin from the fish, ensure no bones remain and cut into bite-size pieces. Cut all the vegetables into bite-size pieces and arrange the gingko nuts on toothpicks (4 to each).

Heat the oil in a large wok to approximately 190° C, dip the pieces of food in the batter and fry until cooked, using long wooden chopsticks to turn occasionally.

When cooked, drain on absorbent paper and transfer to a serving platter. Serve with a side dish of tempura sauce for dipping.

> **Note: It is essential that the oil remains at a constant temperature. The food should be cooked a few pieces at a time and the oil checked regularly and reheated to the original temperature.**

To make the batter, break the eggs into a bowl and add 350 ml ice-cold water. Add the flour and baking soda and mix thoroughly until the batter is smooth and thin, adding a little more ice-cold water if necessary.

> **Note: The correct consistency of batter is essential. It has to be made just prior to using and never stored, even for short periods.**

To make the sauce, heat the mirin in a small saucepan until warm (but not too hot), then remove from the heat and set alight. Shake the pan slightly until the flame dies, then add the soy sauce and dashi (stock) and bring to the boil. Add salt and allow to simmer for 1 minute, then set aside to cool. Finally, add the grated radish, stir to blend and transfer to a side dish.

CHONG YU (steamed pomfret) — *China*

2 dried Chinese mushrooms
1 whole pomfret, approx 800g
4 spring onions, sliced
2 sticks celery, shredded
2 pickled plums, shredded

3 cm knob ginger, finely sliced
2 tsp finely chopped ham
fresh coriander leaves
100 ml chicken stock
3 Tbsp peanut oil

Soak the mushrooms in warm water for 20 minutes, then remove the hard stems and shred the caps. Wash the fish under cold running water and pat dry.

Place the spring onion in a shallow oven-proof dish and lay the fish on top, then arrange the mushroom, celery, pickled plum, ginger, ham and coriander leaves on top. Pour in the stock and place the dish on a steaming rack.

Pour a small quantity of water into a wok and bring to the boil, then set the rack 20 mm above the level of the water. Place a lid on the wok and steam the fish for 10-12 minutes.

Finally, heat the oil until very hot and pour over the fish. Serve immediately.

YAN CANG YU (smoked pomfret)   *Taiwan*

1 whole pomfret,
1 Tbsp finely chopped spring onion
1 Tbsp finely chopped ginger
1 tsp finely chopped garlic
2 Tbsp Chinese wine
2 Tbsp light soy sauce

1 tsp ground anise
1 tsp sugar
175 g ground rice
3 Tbsp dried tea leaves
2 tsp sesame oil

Clean and prepare the fish and score the skin in a criss-cross fashion along both sides. Combine half the onion, ginger, garlic with the wine and soy sauce and rub into the fish. Set aside for 30 minutes, then par-cook in a steamer for 5 minutes and transfer to a rack.

Mix the remaining onion, ginger and garlic with the anise, sugar, rice and tea leaves and transfer to a wok. Place over a high heat until it starts to smoke, then add the rack holding the fish and cover with a tightly fitting lid.

Allow to smoke for 3-4 minutes, then transfer to a serving platter and sprinkle hot sesame oil on top.

TALAKITOK (fish in mango broth)   *Philippines*

500 g whole mackerel
500 g whole red snapper
2 litres rice wash
300 g green mangoes,
  peeled and grated
200 g tomatoes,
  skinned and quartered
100g spring onions, sliced
2 tsp fish sauce

Prepare the fish and cut into slices.

Pour the rice wash into a casserole, add the mango, tomato and spring onion and bring to the boil. Boil for 15 minutes, then add the fish pieces and boil for a further 2 minutes.

Lower heat and simmer for a further few minutes until the fish is fully cooked, then transfer to a soup tureen and serve immediately.

JO LAU YU (fish in wine sauce) — *Hong Kong*

500 g white fish fillets
salt and pepper
1 egg white
2 tsp dark soy sauce
1 Tbsp cornflour
75 g dried wood-ear mushrooms
oil for deep frying
2 tsp sugar
3 Tbsp Chinese wine
125 ml clear fish stock

Cut the fish into serving-size pieces, place in a shallow dish and season with salt and pepper. Whisk the egg white with the soy sauce and half the cornflour and pour over the fish. Stir to coat evenly and set aside for 30 minutes.

Soak the wood-ear mushrooms in warm water for 30 minutes, then rinse under cold running water and pat dry.

Heat the oil in a wok until it starts to smoke and fry the fish for 45 seconds, then remove with a slotted spoon and drain on kitchen paper. Pour away most of the oil and stir-fry the mushrooms for 2 minutes, then add the sugar, wine and stock and bring to the boil.

Mix the remaining cornflour with a small quantity of cold water and stir into the sauce, then replace fish and cook for a further 3 minutes.

CA CHIEN (fish in caramel sauce) — *Vietnam*

4 fillets of white fish, 150 g each
freshly ground black pepper
75 g sugar
2 Tbsp fish sauce

2 Tbsp water
2 tsp finely chopped onion
2 tsp finely chopped garlic

Remove any skin from the fish and season generously with black pepper.

Heat the sugar in a heavy based casserole until it starts to brown, then stir in the fish sauce and water and bring to the boil. Lower heat and allow to simmer for 2-3 minutes, then add the onion and garlic and remove from heat.

Allow to cool, then add the fish, turning to ensure the fillets are evenly coated with sauce. Bring back to the boil, then lower heat, place a lid on the casserole and cook for 15-20 minutes.

SAENGSON CHIM (fish and vegetable stew) *Korea*

600 g firm fish fillets
freshly ground black pepper
2 spring onions, finely chopped
2 tsp finely chopped garlic
2 tsp sugar
2 tsp sesame seeds
1 Tbsp sesame oil

1 large onion, sliced
4 fresh flat mushrooms, sliced
4 carrots, sliced
1 Tbsp chopped chives
1 small red pepper, julienned
25 mm knob fresh ginger, julienned

Remove any skin from the fish and slice the fillets into serving-size pieces, then season with freshly ground pepper.

Mix together the spring onion, garlic, sugar, sesame seeds, sesame oil and half the soy sauce and place in the bottom of an ovenproof casserole.

Add a layer of half the sliced vegetables, then add the fish and sprinkle on the chives. Add the remaining sliced vegetables, then the pepper and ginger.

Mix the remaining soy sauce with the fish stock and pour into the casserole. Bring to the boil, lower heat, cover and cook for 30-35 minutes.

MIRIS MALU (sour spicy fish) *Sri Lanka*

450 g firm fish fillets
0.5 tsp salt
0.25 tsp white pepper
0.25 tsp ground turmeric
50 ml vinegar
2 tsp chopped tamarind

2 tsp finely chopped ginger
2 tsp finely chopped red chilli
1 tsp finely chopped garlic
1 tsp paprika
3 cm cinnamon stick
6 curry leaves

Cut the fish into bite-size pieces, season with salt, pepper and turmeric and set aside for 20 minutes.

Combine the vinegar with an equal quantity of warm water and pour over the tamarind. Leave for 5 minutes, then strain the liquid through a fine sieve and discard the pulp.

Place the fish in a pan and add the ginger, garlic, chilli, paprika, cinnamon stick and curry leaves. Pour in the tamarind liquid and add just sufficient water to barely cover the fish. Bring to the boil, then cover pan, lower heat and allow to simmer for 5-6 minutes.

Remove cover and cook for a further 2 minutes, then discard the cinnamon stick and curry leaves and transfer to a serving dish.

SAKANA NO TSUMEMONO (stuffed red snapper)   *Japan*

4 small red snapper
100 ml sake (rice wine)
2 tsp salt
1 large carrot, finely chopped
3 dried black mushrooms, soaked
* in warm water and finely chopped*
75 g bean curd, finely chopped

1 Tbsp finely chopped spring onion
125 ml clear fish stock
1.5 Tbsp dark soy sauce
2 tsp sugar
2 eggs, lightly beaten
2 Tbsp mirin (sweet rice wine)
16 roasted ginkgo nuts

Cut the fish along the dorsal fin and remove bones. Wash under running water and pat dry, then rub the sake and salt into the cavities.

Place the carrot, mushroom, bean curd, spring onion, sugar, dashi (stock) and half the soy sauce in a small saucepan and bring to the boil. Lower heat and allow to simmer for 4-5 minutes, then add the egg and continue to cook over a low heat, stirring continuously, until the mixture thickens.

Remove pan from heat and allow to cool slightly, then stuff mixture into the fish cavities and bake in a moderate oven for 6-8 minutes, basting occasionally with a mixture of the mirin and remaining soy sauce.

Transfer to a serving plate and garnish with roasted ginkgo nuts

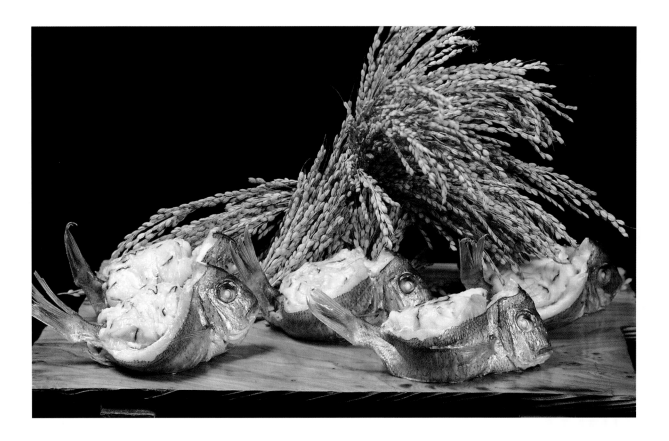

| MEEN POLLICHATU (fish baked in banana leaves) | *India* |

6 small mackerel
banana leaves
4 shallots, chopped
6 cloves garlic, chopped
2 tsp finely chopped ginger
6 fresh green chillies, chopped
8 curry leaves
8 cloves
8 cardamom seeds

12 black peppercorns
8 cm stick cinnamon
grating of nutmeg
1 tsp ground turmeric
1 Tbsp red chilli powder
2 Tbsp vinegar
2 Tbsp coconut oil
salt to taste
1 Tbsp fresh lime juice

Clean and prepare the fish. Cut the banana leaves into 6 squares for wrapping around the fish.

Place the shallots, garlic, ginger, chilli and curry leaves in a blender and blend until smooth. Grind together the cloves, cardamoms, peppercorns, cinnamon and nutmeg and add to the blender together with the turmeric, chilli powder, vinegar, coconut oil and salt. Blend to produce a smooth paste. Coat the fish evenly with the spice paste and set aside for 30 minutes.

Heat the banana leaves over an open fire, then place a fish in the centre of each and wrap securely. Place over a charcoal fire, or under a hot grill, until the fish are cooked, approximately 15 minutes, then unwrap and transfer to a serving platter and sprinkle with lime juice.

GULAI IKAN (fish in spicy coconut sauce)   *Malaysia*

600 g white fish fillets
4 shallots, finely chopped
6 fresh red chillies, finely sliced
1 Tbsp finely chopped ginger
2 tsp finely chopped garlic
2 tsp finely chopped lemon grass
75 ml vegetable oil

0.5 tsp ground coriander
0.5 tsp ground cumin
0.5 tsp ground turmeric
500 ml thin coconut milk
1 Tbsp fresh lime juice
salt to taste
freshly ground black pepper

Cut the fish into serving size pieces. Pound together the shallot, chilli, ginger, garlic and lemon grass to produce a smooth paste.

Heat the oil in a pan and stir-fry the paste for 5 minutes, then add the coriander, cumin, turmeric and coconut milk and bring to the boil.

Stir well and allow to simmer for 5 minutes, then add the fish and season with lime juice, salt and pepper. Cook over a moderate heat, stirring occasionally, until the fish is cooked, then transfer to a serving dish.

Increase the heat and continue to cook until the sauce has reduced, then pour over the fish and serve immediately.

MACHLI KARI (curried fillets of pomfret)   *Pakistan*

600g pomfret fillets
salt and freshly ground black pepper
1 onion, coarsely chopped
75 ml vegetable oil
100 g grated coconut
3 fresh red chillies, finely chopped

1 tsp ground coriander
0.5 tsp ground cumin
0.5 tsp ground turmeric
2 tomatoes,
*   skinned and finely chopped*
1 Tbsp freshly chopped coriander

Remove any skin from the fillets and season with salt and pepper. Heat 2 Tbsp oil in a pan and fry the fillets for 1 minute on each side, then remove. Add the onion to the pan and sauté for 3-4 minutes, then remove.

Wipe the pan, add a further 1 Tbsp oil and stir-fry the coconut for 3 minutes, then place in a mortar, together with the chilli, coriander, cumin and turmeric and pound until smooth.

Add remaining oil to the pan and stir-fry the spice paste for 5 minutes, then add 150 ml of water and bring to the boil. Add the fish and adjust seasonings to taste, then lower heat, cover the pan and cook over a low heat until the fish is cooked, approximately 15 minutes.

Finally, stir in the tomato and heat through, then transfer to a serving plate and garnish with freshly chopped coriander.

JAR SEEN PIN (deep-fried eel)   *Hong Kong*

700 g fresh water eel
1 brown onion, finely chopped
1 carrot, finely chopped
1 stick celery, finely chopped
1 Tbsp finely chopped coriander
1 Tbsp oyster sauce

1 tsp dark soy sauce
1 tsp salt
0.5 tsp freshly ground black pepper
2 Tbsp Chinese wine
2 Tbsp cornflour
oil for deep frying

Wash the eel in hot water and pat dry, then cut into slivers, about 1 cm thick, and place in a shallow dish.

Place the onion, carrot, celery and coriander in a saucepan and cover with 100 mm of water. Bring to the boil and cook until the liquid has reduced by two-thirds, then strain into a bowl and add the oyster sauce, soy sauce, salt, pepper and half the wine. Mix well, then pour over the eel and set aside in the refrigerator for 2 hours, turning occasionally. Remove eel from the marinade and dust with cornflour.

Heat the oil in a wok until very hot and carefully add the eel, one sliver at a time to avoid them sticking together. Cook for 2 minutes, then remove with a slotted spoon and drain on kitchen paper.

Increase the heat until the oil starts to smoke and replace the eel. Cook for a further 30 seconds to make crispy, then remove with a slotted spoon, drain and transfer to a warm platter.

UNAGI UNATAMA (eels with egg sauce)   *Japan*

8 eel fillets
freshly ground black pepper
300 ml Japanese soy sauce

300 ml mirin (sweet rice wine)
100 g soft brown sugar
2 eggs

Carefully skewer each eel fillet with four evenly spaced bamboo skewers, then season with a good grinding of black pepper.

In a saucepan bring the soy sauce and all but 2 Tbsp of the wine to the boil, then add the sugar, lower heat and stir until the sauce is syrupy, then remove pan from heat and set aside for 5 minutes, stirring occasionally.

Coat the eel with sauce and cook under a hot grill for 10-12 minutes, turning once and basting frequently with the remaining sauce, then remove skewers and place the fillets on a bed on steamed rice.

Place the remaining wine in a saucepan, add an equal amount of water and bring to the boil, then break in the eggs and whisk with a fork. When the egg starts to set in strands pour over the eel and serve immediately.

JAR SEEN PIN (deep- fried eel slices)

Poultry

LING MOWN GARP (duck in lemon sauce), *recipe page 86*

LING MENG YA (duck in lemon sauce)   *Singapore*

4 duck breast fillets
4 egg yolks, lightly beaten
3 shallots, finely chopped
2 tsp finely chopped ginger
1.5 Tbsp light soy sauce
1 tsp dark soy sauce
3 Tbsp cornflour
oil for deep frying
fresh lemon slices

Sauce:
2 Tbsp butter
2 Tbsp rice flour
100 ml fresh lemon juice
100 ml chicken stock
2 Tbsp Chinese wine
1 Tbsp sugar
2 tsp cornflour

Remove the skin from the duck fillets and cut the meat into bite size pieces.

Mix together the egg yolks, shallots, ginger, soy sauce and 1 Tbsp cornflour and pour over the duck. Set aside in a cool place for 1 hour, then dust with the remaining cornflour.

Heat the oil in a wok until it starts to smoke, then lower heat slightly, add the duck and cook until tender and crispy. Remove duck and drain on kitchen paper, then arrange on a serving platter and pour on the lemon sauce.

To make the sauce; melt the butter in a saucepan, then remove pan from heat and stir in the flour. Return pan to the heat, add the lemon juice and stock and bring to the boil, then add the wine and sugar and stir to blend.

Finally, mix the cornflour with a small quantity of cold water and stir into the sauce to thicken slightly.

VIT NAU CARI (curried duck)   *Vietnam*

1 dressed duck, about 2 kilos
1 tsp minced garlic
2 tsp finely chopped ginger
2 Tbsp fish sauce
0.5 tsp freshly ground white pepper

2 fresh limes, sliced
4 freshly chopped coriander leaves
2 Tbsp vegetable oil
1 onion, finely chopped
1 Tbsp curry powder

Prepare the duck, then wash and dry thoroughly. Combine the garlic, ginger, fish sauce and pepper and rub inside and over the duck. Set aside for 1 hour, then place the lime and coriander inside the duck and secure with thread.

Roast the duck in a hot oven until tender, then allow to cool before removing the meat and cutting into bite-size slices.

Heat the oil in a wok, add the onion and curry powder and sauté for 2 minutes, then add the duck and cook for 3 minutes, stirring occasionally.

DUM KI BATHAK (spicy duck)   *India*

2 young ducks
250 g natural yoghurt
3 Tbsp cashew nut paste
3 Tbsp almond paste
3 Tbsp ghee
4 cardamoms
4 cloves
1 tsp cumin seeds
3 Tbsp onion paste

4 green chillies, finely chopped
2 Tbsp ginger paste
1 Tbsp garlic paste
10 mint leaves
2 tsp fresh milk
large pinch of saffron
2 Tbsp fresh lemon juice
salt to taste
freshly ground black pepper

Prepare the ducks and cut each into 8 pieces. Whisk the yoghurt and mix with the cashew nut and almond pastes.

Heat the ghee in a large frying pan and add the cardamoms and cloves. When they start to crackle add the onion paste and sauté for 3-4 minutes, then add the chilli and the ginger and garlic pastes and continue to stir for a further 6 minutes.

Add the duck and turn to brown evenly, then add yoghurt and mint leaves. Bring to the boil, then lower heat and allow to simmer for 15 minutes.

Warm the milk, mix with the saffron and add to the pan, then cover pan with a tightly fitting lid. Continue to cook for 20-25 minutes until the duck is tender, then remove lid, add the lemon juice and season to taste with salt and pepper. Stir well and transfer to a large serving dish.

HOU TIN NGARP (crispy roast duck) — *Hong Kong*

1 fat duck, approx. 2.5 kilos
1 Tbsp salt
2 tsp Chinese five-spice powder
125 ml golden syrup
2 Tbsp honey
2 Tbsp light soy sauce
6 spring onions

1 small cucumber
100 ml plum sauce

Pancakes:
500 g plain flour
0.25 tsp salt
75 ml sesame oil

Clean and prepare the duck. Cut off the feet but leave head attached. Immerse the duck in a pan of rapidly boiling water for a few seconds, then remove and pat dry. Rub the salt and five-spice powder inside the duck.

Mix the syrup, honey and soy sauce with a small quantity of water and bring to the boil, then coat the duck, both the inside and the skin, with the syrup mixture.

Place a string around the duck's neck and hang in a cool, draughty place for 4-5 hours to stretch the skin.

> Hanging the duck in front of an electric fan will stretch the skin faster.

Afterwards, place the duck in a moderately hot oven and cook for 2 hours, or until the duck is tender and the skin is crispy and golden, then carve off pieces of skin and arrange on a serving plate.

Cut the spring onions into 5 cm lengths and cut the cucumber into thin sticks. To serve, place a piece of duck on a pancake, add a piece of spring onion and cucumber and top with a little plum sauce. Fold the sides of the pancake over the filling and tuck in the ends to form a secure roll.

To make the pancakes, sift the flour and salt into a bowl and make a well in the centre. Pour in approximately 400 ml boiling water, a little at a time, and mix to form a soft dough. Knead gently for 10 minutes until the dough becomes pliable, then cover and allow to stand for 20-25 minutes.

Turn out on to a lightly-floured surface and shape into a cylinder, approximately 5 cm in diameter, then cut into circles. Brush one side of each circle with sesame oil and place two together with the oiled sides facing, then roll out until they are approximately 15 cm in diameter.

Heat a heavy pan and cook a pair of pancakes for 30-45 seconds on each side, then peel apart and stack on a warm plate until all the pancakes have been cooked.

> As only the outside of the duck is carved for serving with the pancakes, quite a lot of meat remains on the bones. This should be cut off, shredded and stir-fried with vegetables. The carcass can then be used for the preparation of a delicious soup.

LAT JIU KAI HOM (chicken breasts with capsicums) *Hong Kong*

4 boneless chicken breasts
2 egg whites
1.5 Tbsp Chinese wine
2 tsp dark soy sauce
1 tsp sugar
0.5 tsp salt
0.5 tsp freshly ground black pepper
75 ml vegetable oil

1 small red pepper, shredded
1 small green pepper, shredded
2 tsp finely chopped ginger
1 tsp finely chopped garlic
1 Tbsp light soy sauce
1 Tbsp oyster sauce
75 ml chicken stock
2 tsp cornflour

Flatten the chicken breasts slightly with a kitchen mallet and lay in a shallow dish. Beat egg whites with half the wine, soy sauce, sugar, salt and pepper and pour over the chicken, then turn to coat evenly and set aside for 30 minutes.

Heat half the oil in a wok and fry the chicken for 2-3 minutes on each side, then remove to a serving dish and keep warm.

Add half the remaining oil to the wok and stir-fry the peppers for 2 minutes, then remove and arrange on top of the chicken. Add remaining oil and stir-fry the ginger and garlic for 2 minutes, then add the oyster sauce, stock and remaining wine and bring to the boil.

Lower heat and allow to simmer for 2 minutes, then mix the cornflour with a small quantity of cold water and add to the sauce. Stir for a further minute for sauce to thicken slightly, then pour around the chicken and serve immediately.

SHAHI MURG GALOUTI (chicken balls in spiced sauce) *India*

650 g minced chicken breasts
4 green chillies, finely chopped
1 Tbsp finely chopped fresh ginger
2 Tbsp chopped coriander root
2 Tbsp cashew nut paste
2 tsp garam masala
salt to taste
2 Tbsp cornflour
oil for deep frying

2 Tbsp ghee
150 g onions, finely chopped
1 tsp ground turmeric
250 ml chicken stock
75 ml fresh cream
2 Tbsp chopped coriander leaves
large pinch mace
large pinch nutmeg
large pinch ground cardamom

Place the chicken in a bowl, add half the chilli, half the ginger, the coriander root, cashew nut paste, garam masala and salt and blend thoroughly. Divide the mixture and shape into balls, approximately 3 cm in diameter, then dust with the cornflour.

Heat the oil in a pan until it is almost at smoking point and deep fry the chicken balls until golden, then remove with a slotted spoon and drain on kitchen paper.

Pour away most of the oil, then add the ghee and re-heat. Add the onion and remaining chilli and ginger and stir-fry for 2-3 minutes, then add the turmeric and stock and bring to the boil.

Continue to boil over a fairly high heat until the stock is reduced by half, then reduce heat to moderate, add the chicken balls and chopped coriander leaves and stir in the cream. Cook until the sauce reaches coating consistency, then add the mace, nutmeg and cardamom, stir well and transfer to a serving dish.

KHAUKSWE (sautéed chicken with noodles) *Myanmar*

650 g chicken meat
100 g split yellow peas,
  soaked overnight
250 g egg noodles
75 ml vegetable oil
2 onions, chopped
2 tsp finely chopped ginger
2 tsp finely chopped garlic

1 tsp paprika
1 tsp red chilli powder
1 tsp ground turmeric
2 tomatoes, skinned & chopped
salt to taste
freshly ground black pepper
150 ml chicken stock
400 ml thick coconut milk

Boil the chicken for 20 minutes, then chop into bite-size pieces. Cook the peas for 20-25 minutes, or as instructed on the packet. Pour boiling water over the noodles and drain in a colander.

Heat the oil in a saucepan and sauté the onion, ginger and garlic until the onion is translucent, then add the paprika, chilli and turmeric and continue to cook for 2 minutes. Add the chicken and tomato and cook for a further 3-4 minutes, stirring frequently, then add the stock and bring to the boil.

Add the split peas and cover the pan. Lower heat and allow to simmer for 10 minutes, then add the coconut milk. Bring back to the boil, adjust seasonings to taste and stir well, then cook over a moderate heat for 5 minutes.

Meanwhile, cook the noodles in a pan of rapidly boiling water for 3-4 minutes until soft, then drain and transfer to a serving dish. Pour the chicken and sauce on top and garnish with slices of hard boiled eggs.

AYAM BUMBU RUJAK (spicy coconut chicken) *Malaysia*

1 fresh chicken, approx. 1.5 kilos
4 shallots, chopped
8 fresh red chillies, chopped
4 cloves garlic, chopped
1 tsp crumbled shrimp paste

0.5 tsp ground turmeric
1.5 tsp sugar
salt to taste
75 ml vegetable oil
300 ml thick coconut milk

Prepare and disjoint the chicken. Pound the shallot, chilli, garlic, shrimp paste, turmeric, sugar and salt together with a small quantity of the oil to produce a smooth paste.

Heat remaining oil in a large pan and stir-fry the spice-paste for 10 minutes, then add the chicken, coconut milk and 200 ml water.

Bring to a boil, then lower heat and cook for 40-50 minutes, stirring frequently, until the chicken is tender and the sauce has thickened.

TANDOORI MURG (barbecued chicken) *India*

2 chickens, approx. 1 kilo each
75 ml fresh lemon juice
2 tsp salt
200 g natural yoghurt
2 Tbsp ginger paste
2 Tbsp garlic paste
1 Tbsp red chilli powder
1 Tbsp green chilli pepper
2 tsp garam masala
2 tsp ground cumin
2 Tbsp groundnut oil
few drops of orange colouring
soft butter for basting

Remove skin from the chickens and with a sharp knife make a number of deep incisions in the flesh, 3 on each breast, 3 on each thigh and 2 on each drum stick. Sprinkle half the lemon juice over the chickens and rub in the salt.

Whisk the yoghurt in a bowl, add all the remaining ingredients apart from the butter and blend thoroughly. Pour the mixture over the chickens and set aside in the refrigerator for 5 hours, turning occasionally.

Remove chickens from marinade and place in a roasting tin or ,alternatively, if the oven has a rotisserie, thread on a skewer. (In either case ensure chickens are not touching each other.)

Cook in a pre-heated hot oven for 12-15 minutes, basting frequently with the butter, then cut into pieces, transfer to a serving dish and garnish with slices of onion and tomato.

GAI XAO GUNG (chicken with ginger) *Vietnam*

4 chicken thighs
3 cm knob ginger, finely sliced
2 fresh red chillies, finely sliced
3 Tbsp fish sauce

2 Tbsp vegetable oil
1 tsp hoi sin sauce
1 tsp sesame oil
1 Tbsp finely sliced spring onion

Chop the chicken into bite-size pieces and rinse to remove any bone splinters.

Combine the ginger, chilli and fish sauce and pour over the chicken. Turn to coat evenly, then set aside for 1 hour.

Heat the oil in a wok, add the chicken with marinade and the hoi sin sauce. Stir-fry for 10 minutes, then cover and cook until the chicken is tender.

Transfer to a serving dish, sprinkle with hot sesame oil and garnish with onion.

RELLENONG MANOK (stuffed chicken)   *Philippines*

1 fresh chicken, approx. 1.25 kilos
1 tsp sea salt
0.5 tsp freshly ground white pepper
150 g garlic sausage, chopped
350 g minced pork
100 g onions, finely chopped
100 g can pimentos, finely sliced
50 g stuffed olives, finely sliced
50 g raisins
50 g grated Edam cheese
2 eggs, lightly beaten
50 g butter

Clean and prepare the chicken and carefully de-bone, then rub salt and pepper inside and over the skin. Mix together all the remaining ingredients, apart from the butter, and adjust seasonings to taste, then stuff inside the chicken. Wrap thin strips of foil around the chicken to maintain the shape and secure opening with kitchen thread.

Melt the butter and brush over the chicken and bake in a pre-heated, moderate oven for at least 1 hour until the chicken is cooked and the skin is golden brown.

Slice and serve immediately with fresh vegetables, or allow to cool before slicing and serve with a green salad.

PANAENG GAI (dry chicken curry)   *Thailand*

4 chicken breast fillets
salt & freshly ground black pepper
3 Tbsp plain flour
75 ml vegetable oil
2 Tbsp hot curry paste

250 ml thick coconut milk
3 Tbsp chopped roasted peanuts
2 Tbsp fish sauce
1 Tbsp sugar
fresh basil leaves

Cut the chicken into slices, season with salt and pepper and dust with flour.

Heat the oil in a wok and sauté the chicken until well browned, then remove and drain on kitchen paper. Pour away most of the oil and reheat the wok, then add the curry paste and stir for 2 minutes.

Add the coconut milk, bring to the boil and retain over a moderate heat until the liquid has reduced by half, then replace the chicken, add the peanuts, fish sauce and sugar and stir well.

Cook over a fairly high heat until the chicken is tender and almost dry, then transfer to a serving dish and garnish with basil leaves.

JIAO HUA JI (baked stuffed chicken)   *China*

1 whole chicken, approx. 1.5 kilos
2 tsp salt
6 dried Chinese mushrooms
2 Tbsp vegetable oil
125 g minced pork
100 g pickled cabbage, shredded
100 g beetroot, shredded
1 large brown onion, chopped
2 spring onions, chopped

3 cm knob ginger, finely chopped
2 Tbsp Chinese wine
1 Tbsp light soy sauce
1 tsp dark soy sauce
freshly ground black pepper
2 tsp sesame oil
lotus leaves (optional)
500 g shortcrust pastry dough

Clean and prepare the chicken and rub the skin and the inside with salt, then set aside. Soak the mushrooms in warm water for 20 minutes, then discard the hard stems and shred the caps.

Heat the oil in a wok and stir-fry the pork for 2 minutes, then add vegetables, wine, soy sauce and pepper and cook over a moderate heat for 2-3 minutes, stirring frequently.

Stir in the sesame oil, then remove mixture with a slotted spoon and set aside to cool, then stuff into the chicken. Wrap the chicken in lotus leaves (if using) and encase in the pastry dough.

Bake in a moderately slow oven, until the chicken is tender, about 3 hours, then discard the dough and leaves and transfer to a serving plate.

AYAM GORENG (fried chicken) — *Malaysia*

1 chicken, about 1.5 kilos
4 shallots
4 fresh red chillies
2 tsp finely chopped ginger
1 tsp finely chopped garlic
1 tsp finely chopped lemon grass

1 tsp curry powder
0.25 tsp ground turmeric
150 ml thick coconut milk
salt to taste
freshly ground black pepper
oil for deep frying

Prepare and joint the chicken, season with lime juice, salt and pepper and place in a shallow dish. Pound the shallot, chilli, ginger, garlic, lemon grass, curry powder, turmeric and sugar to produce a smooth paste.

Add the coconut milk to the paste and stir to blend thoroughly, then pour over the chicken and set aside in the refrigerator for 1 hour.

Heat 2 Tbsp oil in a wok and add the chicken together with the marinade. Cook over a fairly high heat until the chicken is almost tender and the liquid has been absorbed, then remove and drain on kitchen paper.

Heat remaining oil in a clean wok until it starts to smoke, then add the chicken and cook for 2-3 minutes, until the skin is golden and crispy. Remove, drain off excess oil and serve with a hot chilli dip.

96

KARI KERING HATI AYAM (chicken liver curry) *Malaysia*

400 g chicken livers
3 Tbsp sunflower oil
2 shallots, finely chopped
2 tsp finely chopped fresh ginger
1 tsp finely chopped garlic
2 cloves

8 cm cinnamon stick
1 tsp ground anise
1 tsp ground cumin
1 tsp freshly ground white pepper
salt to taste
225 ml thick coconut milk

Wash the chicken livers under cold running water, then pat dry.

Heat the oil in a pan and stir-fry the shallot, ginger and garlic for 3 minutes, then add the cloves, cinnamon, anise, cumin, pepper and salt and continue to cook over a fairly high heat for a further 3 minutes.

Add the chicken livers and cook for 15-20 minutes, stirring occasionally, then pour in the coconut milk and bring to the boil.

Cook until the liquid has almost completely reduced, then remove cinnamon stick and cloves and transfer to a serving dish.

YIM KUK GAI GON (chicken livers baked in salt) *Hong Kong*

400 g chicken livers
2 shallots, finely chopped
2 spring onions, finely chopped
2 tsp finely chopped ginger
2 tsp crushed garlic
3 Tbsp Chinese wine

1 Tbsp light soy sauce
2 tsp dark soy sauce
1 tsp sugar
0.5 tsp freshly ground white pepper
1 kilo rock salt

Wash the chicken livers under cold running water, then pat dry.

Combine the shallot, onion, ginger, garlic, wine, soy sauce, sugar and pepper and sprinkle over the livers. Set aside for 30 minutes

Heat the rock salt in a wok until it is extremely hot, then transfer half to a fresh hot wok and lay the chicken livers on top. Cover with remaining hot salt and place a tightly fitting lid on the wok. Bake for 15-20 minutes.

Note: If personal preference dictates a longer cooking time, always reheat the salt before proceeding.

YIM KUK GUP (pigeons baked in salt)   *Hong Kong*

2 plump pigeons
4 shallots, finely chopped
4 spring onions, finely chopped
25 mm ginger, finely chopped
4 cloves garlic, finely chopped
0.5 tsp ground anise

0.5 tsp Chinese five-spice powder
2 Tbsp Chinese wine
1.5 Tbsp light soy sauce
2 tsp dark soy sauce
0.5 tsp freshly ground white pepper
2 kilos rock salt

Prepare the pigeons. Combine together all the remaining ingredients, apart from the rock salt, and stuff inside the pigeons. Set aside for 1 hour, then wrap the birds individually in well-oiled baking parchment.

Heat the rock salt in a wok until it is extremely hot, then transfer half to a fresh preheated wok, add the pigeons and cover with remaining salt. Place a tightly-fitting lid on the wok and set aside for 10-12 minutes. Remove birds and re-heat the salt, then repeat the process.

To serve, unwrap and chop the pigeons into bite-size pieces.

JING GUP ZONG (steamed minced pigeon)   *Taiwan*

2 plump pigeons
175 g fat pork
75 g water chestnuts
4 spring onions, finely chopped
1 tsp finely chopped ginger
2 tsp minced garlic

1 Tbsp Chinese wine
1 Tbsp light soy sauce
2 tsp dark soy sauce
1 tsp freshly ground black pepper
150 ml chicken stock

Prepare the pigeons, remove bones and cut the meat into small chunks. Chop the pork and chestnuts, combine with the meat and pass through a fine mincer.

Add all the remaining ingredients and stir to combine thoroughly, then divide the mixture into four heat-proof cups.

Place the cups in a tightly sealed container and steam over rapidly boiling water for 4-5 minutes. Serve immediately

CHAU GARP SOWN (minced pigeon in lettuce leaves) — *Hong Kong*

2 plump pigeons
100 g chicken livers
2 eggs
2 Tbsp light soy sauce
1 Tbsp cornflour
1 tsp sugar
0.5 tsp freshly ground black

4 Tbsp peanut oil
75 g bamboo shoots, finely chopped
3 spring onions, finely chopped
2 tsp finely chopped ginger
2 Tbsp Chinese wine
2 tsp oyster sauce
lettuce leaves

Clean and prepare the pigeons and boil for 30-35 minutes, until tender, then allow to cool, de-bone and place through a coarse mincer. Blanch the chicken livers in boiling water, then chop finely and add to the meat. Beat the eggs with the soy sauce, cornflour, sugar and pepper and pour over the meat. Set aside for 20 minutes, then remove with a slotted spoon and drain. Reserve the marinade.

Soak the mushrooms in warm water for 20 minutes, then discard the hard stems and finely chop the caps.

Heat the oil in a wok, add the bamboo shoot, mushroom, spring onion and ginger and stir-fry for 2 minutes, then add the wine, oyster sauce and marinade and bring to the boil. Add the meat, adjust seasonings, and cook for a further 3 minutes.

To serve, spoon individual portions onto crispy lettuce leaves and add a little plunb sauce.

Meat

GOSHT SHAB KORMA (spiced lamb with apples), *recipe page 102*

GOSHT SHAB KORMA (spiced lamb with apples) *Pakistan*

2 lamb neck fillets
2 cooking apples,
  peeled, cored and diced
3 Tbsp ghee
1 large brown onion, chopped
2 ripe tomatoes,
  skinned, seeded and mashed
2 tsp finely chopped garlic

2 tsp ground coriander
1 tsp ground cumin
1 tsp red chilli powder
2 Tbsp ground cashew nuts
75 g natural yoghurt
salt to taste
freshly ground black pepper
50 ml fresh cream

Trim excess fat from the meat and cut into small chunks. Peel, core and dice the apples.

Heat the ghee in a pan, add the onion and fry until translucent, then add the tomato, garlic, coriander and cumin and stir-fry for 5 minutes. Add the cashew nuts and chilli powder and cook for 3 minutes, then add the yoghurt, season to taste with salt and pepper and bring to the boil.

Lower the heat and allow to simmer for 5 minutes, then add the lamb, pour in 225 ml cold water and bring back to the boil. Again, lower the heat and cook slowly for 20-25 minutes, then add the apple and continue to cook until the lamb is tender.

Remove pan from the heat, stir in the cream and transfer to a serving dish.

KAMBING BUMBU BACEM (spicy boiled lamb) *Indonesia*

1 kilo shoulder of lamb
1 large onion, sliced
2 tsp crushed garlic
1 tsp red chilli powder
2 tsp brown sugar

1 Tbsp tamarind pulp
2 tsp ground coriander
1 tsp finely chopped ginger
1 kaffir lime leaf
salt to taste

Place the lamb in a large saucepan and add the onion and garlic, then add just sufficient cold water to cover and bring to the boil.

Add remaining ingredients, then lower heat and cook over a moderate heat until the lamb is tender. Remove the meat and allow to cool, then cut into thick slices and place in a fresh pan.

Strain the cooking stock over the meat and bring back to the boil, then lower heat and cook until the sauce has reduced by half. Serve immediately.

GULAI KAMBING (spicy lamb stew)   *Indonesia*

850 g shoulder of lamb, boned
1 onion, chopped
3 fresh red chillies, chopped
2 tsp chopped ginger
1 tsp chopped garlic
1 tsp chopped lemon grass
1 tsp chopped coriander root
4 macadamia nuts
2 tsp sugar
1 litre thick coconut milk

2 Tbsp vegetable oil
0.5 tsp ground cardamom
0.5 tsp ground cumin
0.5 tsp ground turmeric
0.5 tsp ground fennel
salt to taste
5 cm stick cinnamon
4 cloves
2 bay leaves

Trim the lamb and cut into bite-size chunks. In a mortar, pound together the onion, chilli, ginger, garlic, lemon grass, coriander root, macadamia nuts, sugar and pepper with 2 Tbsp coconut milk to produce a smooth paste.

Heat the oil in a pan and stir-fry the paste for 2 minutes, then add the meat and continue to cook, stirring frequently, for a further 3 minutes. Add the cardamom, cumin, turmeric, fennel, salt, cinnamon stick and cloves and stir well, then pour in the remaining coconut milk and bring to the boil.

Lower heat and allow to simmer, stirring occasionally, for about 45 minutes, or until the lamb is very tender. Remove the bay leaves and cinnamon stick, then transfer to a warm dish and serve with steamed rice.

KOLA URUNDAI (minced lamb patties) *India*

750 g minced lamb
6 fresh green chillies, chopped
6 spring onions, chopped
6 roasted curry leaves
1 Tbsp finely chopped ginger
2 tsp finely chopped garlic
1.5 tsp ground anise
2 Tbsp chopped cashew nuts
3 Tbsp roasted lentils
2 eggs, lightly beaten

Sauce:
3 Tbsp chopped cashew nuts
3 Tbsp freshly grated coconut
75 ml vegetable oil
6 green cardamom seeds
1 tsp cumin seeds
4 fresh green chillies, chopped
3 tomatoes, skinned and chopped
100 ml fresh cream

Place three-quarters of the lamb in a pan, cover with water and bring to the boil. Boil for 5 minutes, then remove, drain and place in a large mixing bowl.

Add remaining meat, chilli, onion, curry leaves, ginger, garlic, anise, cashew nuts and lentils and pound until smooth, then add the egg, Mix to blend, then divide mixture into small balls, approximately 3 cm in diameter and place in the refrigerator for 1 hour.

Meanwhile, prepare the sauce: grind the cashew nuts with a small quantity of cold water to produce a smooth paste and do likewise with the coconut.

Heat the oil in a pan until it starts to smoke and add the cardamoms and cumin seeds. When they start to crackle add the cashew paste, coconut paste and chilli and lower the heat. Continue to cook for 10 minutes, stirring frequently, then add the tomato and cook for a further 5 minutes. Finally, add the cream, remove pan from heat and stir to blend.

Replace pan on the heat, add the meatballs and bring to a low boil. Allow to simmer for 5-6 minutes, then transfer to a warm dish and serve immediately.

CONG BAO YANG ROU (stir-fried lamb with leeks)   *China*

300 g lamb neck fillet
3 Tbsp Chinese wine
2 Tbsp light soy sauce
2 tsp dark soy sauce
0.5 tsp freshly ground white pepper
3 Tbsp vegetable oil
1 Tbsp finely chopped ginger
2 tsp minced garlic
4 leeks, sliced diagonally
75 ml chicken stock
2 tsp sesame oil

Cut the lamb into thin, bite-size pieces and place in a shallow dish. Mix the wine, soy sauce and pepper and pour over the lamb. Set aside for 30 minutes, turning the meat occasionally.

Heat the oil in a wok until it starts to smoke, then lower heat slightly and add the ginger and garlic. Stir-fry for 1 minute, then add the leek and continue to stir for a further minute.

Add the lamb together with the marinade and cook for 2 minutes, then add the stock and vinegar and bring to the boil. Lower heat to a simmer, add the sesame oil and stir well, then transfer to a large dish and serve immediately.

XIANG CUI YANG ROU (crispy lamb)   *China*

800 g boned leg of lamb
25 mm knob ginger, finely sliced
3 cloves garlic
10 Szechuan peppercorns
0.5 tsp ground anise
1 Tbsp sugar

2 Tbsp light soy sauce
2 tsp dark soy sauce
1 Tbsp vinegar
2 eggs
peanut oil for deep frying

Cut the lamb into bite-size chunks, place in a wok and cover with water. Bring to the boil and simmer for 3 minutes, then remove and rinse under cold water.

Clean the wok and replace the meat. Add the ginger, garlic, peppercorns and just sufficient water to cover the meat by approximately 25 mm. Bring to the boil, add the anise, sugar, soy sauce and vinegar, and cook over a moderate heat until the lamb is tender, then remove, drain and place in a shallow dish.

Whisk the eggs lightly together with the cornflour and pour over the meat, then stir to coat evenly.

Heat the oil in a wok until it starts to smoke, then add the meat and fry until the outside is crispy. Remove and drain off excess oil.

PAAD LOOG CHIN (fried pork balls & vegetables) *Thailand*

550 g pork loin
2 dried black mushrooms
1 tsp minced garlic
1 tsp finely chopped coriander root
1 tsp sugar
0.5 tsp salt
0.5 tsp freshly ground black pepper

1 Tbsp fresh lime juice
1 egg, lightly beaten
2 shallots, finely chopped
2 water chestnuts, finely chopped
75 g bamboo shoots, finely chopped
2 Tbsp plain flour
oil for deep frying

Trim any excess fat from the pork and place through a mincer. In a mixing bowl, pound together the garlic, coriander root, sugar, salt, pepper and lime juice to produce a smooth paste. Add the pork and egg, blend thoroughly and set aside for 30 minutes. Soak the mushrooms in warm water for 20 minutes, then discard the hard stems and finely chop the caps.

Add the mushroom, shallot, water chestnut, bamboo shoot and flour to the pork and mix well, then shape into small balls, approximately 3 cm in diameter.

Heat the oil in a wok until it starts to smoke, then reduce heat, add the pork balls and fry for 6-8 minutes. Remove with a slotted spoon, drain on kitchen paper and serve on a bed of freshly cooked vegetables.

MENUDO (diced pork with chick peas) *Philippines*

400 g lean pork diced
200 g pork liver, thinly sliced
0.5 tsp salt
0.5 tsp freshly ground white pepper
200 g chick peas, soaked
2 Tbsp corn oil

1 onion, finely chopped
4 cloves garlic, finely chopped
2 tomatoes, skinned and chopped
2 potatoes, diced
1 red pepper, seeded and chopped
100 ml vegetable or chicken stock

Blanch the pork and liver in separate pans for 1 minute, then season with salt and pepper and set aside to cool. Cook the chick peas until tender, then drain and allow to cool.

Heat the oil in a pan and saute the onion and garlic for 3-4 minutes, then add the tomato and cook until soft and mushy.

Add the pork and continue to stir for 3 minutes, then add potato, red pepper and stock and bring to the boil. Simmer until the pork is tender, then add the liver and chick peas and adjust seasonings to taste.

Continue to cook for a further 2-3 minutes, then transfer to a warm dish and serve immediately.

CRISPY PATA (deep fried pig's trotters) *Philippines*

4 pig's trotters
2 tsp crushed garlic
0.5 tsp salt
0.5 tsp freshly ground white pepper
oil for deep frying

Sauce:
2 tsp finely chopped garlic
2 Tbsp fresh calamansi juice
1 Tbsp light soy sauce
0.5 tsp freshly ground white pepper

Wash the trotters under cold running water and pat dry, then place in a large pot, add the garlic, salt and pepper and cover with water.

Bring to the boil, then lower heat, place a tightly-fitting lid on the pot and allow to simmer for approximately 3 hours, until the meat is very tender. Remove and set aside to cool.

Heat the oil in a deep pan until it starts to smoke, then add the trotters and cook until the skin is crispy. Remove, drain off excess oil and serve immediately with a side dish of dipping sauce.

To make the sauce; combine the garlic, calamansi juice, soy sauce and pepper and stir to blend thoroughly.

SUEN TIM GOR YUK (sweet & sour pork rolls)   *Hong Kong*

300 g pork fillet
150 g pork fat, finely chopped
150 g water chestnuts, chopped
2 Tbsp freshly chopped coriander
2 tsp sugar
1 tsp Chinese five-spice powder
0.5 tsp salt
0.5 tsp freshly ground black pepper
1 Tbsp cornflour

200 ml peanut oil
1 small red pepper, chopped
1 small green pepper, chopped
100 g pineapple chunks
100 ml rice vinegar
2 Tbsp tomato ketchup
2 tsp dark soy sauce
1 Tbsp sesame seeds

Trim the meat and cut into fine shreds, then mix with the pork fat, chestnut, coriander, sugar, five-spice powder, salt and pepper. Lay the mixture on a piece of muslin and shape into a roll, approximately 25 mm in diameter. Cook in a steamer for 10 minutes, then allow to cool, cut into 25 mm pieces and dust with the cornflour.

Heat the oil in a wok and fry the rolls for 2-3 minutes, until golden, then remove and drain on kitchen paper. Pour away most of the oil and reheat the wok. Add the peppers and stir-fry for 2 minutes, then add the vinegar, ketchup and soy sauce, adjust seasonings to taste and bring to the boil.

Lower heat slightly, add the pineapple and replace the pork. Stir for a further 2 minutes, then transfer to a serving dish and sprinkle the sesame seeds on top.

URU VINDALOO (hot & sour pork curry)   *Sri Lanka*

700 g lean pork
50 ml vinegar
1 onion, finely chopped
2.5 cm knob ginger, finely chopped
6 cloves garlic, finely chopped
6 red chillies, finely chopped

12 black peppercorns
2 tsp cumin seeds
3 Tbsp vegetable oil
1 tsp mustard seeds
2 tomatoes, quartered
1 tsp ground turmeric

Cut the pork into bite-size cubes. Mix 1 Tbsp vinegar with 200 ml cold water and rinse the pork. Pound together the onion, ginger, garlic, chilli, peppercorns, cumin and remaining vinegar and rub over the pork. Set aside for 30 minutes.

Heat the oil in a pan and sauté the pork for 5 minutes, then add the tomato and turmeric and pour in sufficient hot water to cover.

Cover the pan and cook until the pork is tender, then transfer to a bowl and serve with steamed rice.

SUEN TIM GOR YUK (sweet and sour pork rolls)

MOO GROB (crispy fried pork) — *Thailand*

325 g whole piece pork belly
1 tsp salt
oil for deep frying
3 shallots, finely chopped
2 fresh red chillies, finely sliced
2 fresh green chillies, finely sliced
25 mm knob ginger, shredded
2 tsp minced garlic
2 tomatoes, skinned & chopped

1 tsp chopped coriander root
1 Tbsp rice wine
1 Tbsp light soy sauce
2 tsp dark soy sauce
50 ml chicken stock
freshly ground black pepper
2 tsp fish sauce
freshly chopped coriander leaves

With a sharp knife score the skin of the pork every 15 mm and rub in the salt. Set aside for 45 minutes, then cut into strips. Heat the oil in a wok until it starts to smoke and fry the pork until the skin is crispy and golden, then remove with a slotted spoon and drain on kitchen paper. Let cool, then cut into small pieces.

Pour away most of the oil, re-heat the wok and stir-fry the shallot, ginger and garlic for 3-4 minutes, then add the chilli, tomato, coriander root, wine, soy sauce and stock and bring to the boil.

Add the pork, season to taste with pepper, lower heat and allow to simmer for 15 minutes, stirring occasionally. Finally, add the fish sauce, stir well and cook for a further 3 minutes, then transfer to a serving dish and garnish with freshly chopped coriander leaves.

RISHAD GOAN (spiced pork chops) — *India*

8 pork chops
4 fresh green chillies, chopped
6 cloves garlic, finely chopped
2 Tbsp red chilli paste
2 Tbsp ginger paste
1.5 tsp ground turmeric

1 Tbsp roasted ground cumin
0.5 tsp salt
2 tsp freshly ground black pepper
3 Tbsp vinegar
2 Tbsp olive oil
freshly chopped coriander leaves

Trim excess fat from the chops and arrange on a large tray. Mix the green chilli, garlic, chilli paste, ginger paste, turmeric, cumin, salt, pepper and vinegar and pound to produce a coarse paste. Spread the paste over the chops and set aside for 30 minutes.

Place in a lightly-oiled roasting tray and bake in a pre-heated, moderate oven until well cooked, then transfer to a serving platter and garnish with freshly chopped coriander.

HUI WO ROU (twice cooked pork with vegetables) *China*

450 g pork loin
oil for deep frying
3 spring onions, chopped
3 sticks celery, chopped
1 green pepper, chopped
2 fresh red chillies, finely sliced
2 tsp minced garlic
1.5 Tbsp chilli bean paste
0.5 tsp sugar
0.5 tsp freshly ground black pepper
1 Tbsp Chinese wine
1 Tbsp light soy sauce
1 tsp dark soy sauce
75 ml chicken stock
1 tsp cornflour

Immerse the pork in a pan of boiling water, then lower heat and allow to simmer until the pork is fully cooked, approximately 1¼ hours. Remove pork and allow to cool, then cut into thin slices.

Heat the oil in a wok until very hot and deep-fry the pork until crispy, then remove with a slotted spoon and drain on kitchen paper. Pour away most of the oil and re-heat the wok, then add the onion, celery, pepper, chilli and garlic and stir-fry for 3 minutes.

Add the bean paste, sugar, pepper, wine, soy sauce and stock and bring to the boil. Lower heat and replace the pork, then continue to cook over a moderate heat, stirring frequently, for a further 2 minutes.

Finally, mix the cornflour with a small quantity of cold water and stir into the sauce to thicken slightly, then transfer to a warm dish and serve immediately.

HEO CHUA NGOT (glazed pork) *Vietnam*

450 g pork, cut into bite-size chunks
1 large onion, chopped
2 tsp finely chopped garlic
3 Tbsp vegetable oil

3 Tbsp soft brown sugar
3 Tbsp fish sauce
0.5 tsp freshly ground black pepper

Cut the pork into bite-size chunks. Heat the oil in a cooking pot and stir-fry the onion and garlic for 3 minutes, then add the pork and stir until it starts to brown.

Add the sugar, fish sauce, pepper and 1 litre of water and bring to the boil, then simmer until the pork is tender and the liquid has reduced and become syrupy.

LOH BAK NGOU NAM BOU
(braised beef and turnips)

Hong Kong

650 g beef topside
0.5 tsp salt
0.25 tsp freshly ground black pepper
3 Tbsp vegetable oil
3 cm knob ginger, thinly sliced
2 tsp finely chopped garlic
2 tsp finely chopped red chilli
1 Tbsp soybean paste

300 g turnips,
*   cut into bite-size wedges*
1 Tbsp Chinese wine
1 Tbsp light soy sauce
2 tsp dark soy sauce
1 Tbsp oyster sauce
1 tsp sugar
1 Tbsp cornflour

Cut the beef into large chunks and season with salt and pepper. Heat half the oil in a wok and stir-fry the beef to seal completely, then remove and drain.

Heat the remaining oil in a clay cooking pot, add the ginger, garlic, chilli and soybean and stir-fry for 3 minutes, then add the beef and cook for a further 2 minutes. Add sufficient water to barely cover the beef and bring to the boil, then place a tightly-fitting lid on the pot and lower the heat.

Cook slowly for 90 minutes, then remove the lid, add the sugar, wine, soy sauce and oyster sauce and bring back to the boil. Add the turnip and simmer for 15 minutes.

Mix the cornflour with a little cold water and stir into the pot to thicken the sauce, then serve immediately.

GYRUNIKU TEPPANYAKI (fried beef with garlic) — *Japan*

600 g fillet steak
1 tsp sugar
1 tsp freshly ground black pepper
100 ml mirin (sweet rice wine)
100 ml shoyu (Japanese soy sauce)

8 cloves garlic, finely chopped
2 Tbsp shredded white radish
2 tsp finely chopped ginger
2 tsp sugar

Cut the beef into bite-size pieces and place in a dish. Season with pepper and add the wine and soy sauce. Stir and set aside for 30 minutes, then remove meat from the marinade and drain on kitchen paper. Reserve marinade.

Pour a little oil on to an open griddle (or large frying pan) and fry the garlic until it is golden and crispy, then push to one side.

Add a little more oil to the griddle and fry the meat for 3-4 minutes (or longer if preferred), turning frequently and basting occasionally with a little marinade, then mix with the crispy fried garlic and transfer to a serving platter.

Combine the radish, ginger and sugar with the remaining marinade and serve as a dipping sauce.

DAGING RAGI (beef with shredded coconut) — *Malaysia*

500 g rump steak
0.5 tsp salt
0.5 tsp freshly ground black pepper
3 Tbsp vegetable oil
1 onion, finely chopped
1 tsp finely chopped garlic

2 tsp finely chopped lemon grass
0.5 tsp ground coriander
200 ml thick coconut milk
25 ml tamarind water
75 g shredded coconut
2 tsp finely chopped roasted peanuts

Cut the beef into bite-size pieces and season with salt and pepper.

Heat the oil in a pan and sauté the onion, garlic and lemon grass for 3 minutes, then add the beef and coriander and stir until the meat is completely sealed.

Add the coconut milk and tamarind water and bring to the boil, then lower heat and cook until the liquid has reduced by half.

Add the shredded coconut and continue to cook, stirring frequently until most of the liquid has been absorbed, then transfer to a serving dish and sprinkle the peanuts on top.

BANH MI BO KHO (beef stew) — *Vietnam*

800 g stewing steak
2 shallots, finely chopped
1 Tbsp finely chopped ginger
2 tsp minced garlic
1 tsp finely chopped lemon grass
1 tsp sugar
0.5 tsp freshly ground black pepper
50 ml light soy sauce
2 tsp dark soy sauce

50 ml vegetable oil
1 onion, chopped
1 tomato, skinned & chopped
1 Tbsp chilli paste
1 Tbsp fish sauce
3 carrots, cut into bite-size chunks
1 sweet potato,
  cut into bite-size chunks

Trim the beef, cut into 30 mm chunks and place in a bowl. Mix together the shallot, chilli, ginger, half the garlic, the lemon grass, sugar, pepper and soy sauce and add to the beef. Stir well and place in the refrigerator for 1 hour.

Heat half the oil in a large pan, add the beef and stir-fry for 2 minutes, then remove with a slotted spoon and drain on kitchen paper. Heat the remaining oil in the pan, add the onion and remaining garlic and stir-fry for 2-3 minutes, then add the tomato, chilli paste and fish sauce and replace the beef.

Cook for 5 minutes, then pour in 1.5 litres of water and bring to the boil. Stir well, then lower heat, cover the pan and allow to simmer for 1-1¼ hour. Add the carrot and sweet potato and retain over a low heat until the meat is tender and the vegetables cooked. Serve immediately.

JUNK CHOW CHEN JIU NGOU YOK SZE
(shredded beef in taro nests)

Hong Kong

300 g shredded beef
0.5 tsp salt
0.25 tsp freshly ground black pepper
0.25 tsp five-spice powder
2 Tbsp Chinese wine
300 g taro root, peeled and shredded
1 egg, lightly beaten
3 Tbsp cornflour
vegetable oil for deep frying
1 onion, finely chopped
1 small green pepper, shredded
2 fresh red chillies, shredded
2 tsp finely chopped ginger
1 tsp finely chopped garlic
1 tsp sugar
2 Tbsp light soy sauce
2 tsp dark soy sauce
2 tsp oyster sauce
50 ml beef stock

Place the beef in a shallow dish, season with salt, pepper, five-spice powder and wine and set aside for 20 minutes, stirring occasionally.

Whisk the egg with half the cornflour and mix with the shredded taro. Divide the taro into six portions and arrange each between two small wire baskets. Heat the oil in a wok until it starts to smoke, then submerge the wire baskets and fry for minutes until golden and crispy. Drain on kitchen paper, then take the taro from the baskets, arrange on a platter and place in a warming oven.

Wipe the wok clean, add 3 Tbsp oil and re-heat. Add the beef and stir-fry for 1 minute, then remove with a slotted spoon. Add the onion, pepper, chilli, ginger and garlic and stir-fry for 2-3 minutes, then add the sugar, soy sauce, oyster sauce and stock and bring to the boil. Replace the beef and cook for a further 2 minutes.

Mix the remaining cornflour with a little cold water, add to the wok and stir to thicken, then spoon the beef into the taro 'nests' and serve immediately.

Notes: * If difficulty is found in obtaining taro root a very starchy variety of potato could be substituted. *For a Chinese meal, with a number of dishes being place on the table simultaneously, one larger 'nest' might be thought more appropriate. *Other stir-fry dishes would make suitable fillings but they should always be fairly dry.

HO YAU NGAU YUK (beef in oyster sauce) *Hong Kong*

4 dried Chinese mushrooms
400 g lean beef
1 egg white
2 Tbsp Chinese wine
1 Tbsp light soy sauce
2 tsp cornflour
0.5 tsp freshly ground black pepper

3 Tbsp peanut oil
1 carrot, shredded
2 tsp finely chopped ginger
1 tsp minced garlic
1 Tbsp finely sliced spring onion
3 Tbsp oyster sauce

Soak the mushrooms in warm water for 20 minutes, then discard the hard stems and shred the caps. Cut the beef into thin, bite-size pieces and place in a shallow dish. Beat the egg-white with the wine, soy sauce, cornflour and pepper and pour over the meat, then set aside for 30 minutes.

Heat the oil in a wok, add the ginger and garlic and stir-fry for 2 minutes, then add the carrot and mushroom and continue to stir for a further minute. Add the beef together with the marinade and bring to the boil.

Stir for 1 minute, then add the spring onion and oyster sauce and adjust seasonings to taste. Bring back to the boil and stir for a further 30-45 seconds, then transfer to a warm dish and serve immediately.

KALBI CHIM (beef ribs with water chestnuts)   *Korea*

1.25 kilos meaty beef ribs
75 ml rice wine
75 ml light soy sauce
2 tsp dark soy sauce
2 tsp sesame oil
2 Tbsp finely chopped shallot
1 Tbsp finely chopped spring onion
1 Tbsp finely chopped ginger
2 tsp finely chopped garlic

1.5 Tbsp toasted sesame seeds
1 Tbsp sugar
1 tsp freshly ground black pepper
75 ml vegetable oil
2 onions, sliced
2 tomatoes, sliced
75 g canned water chestnuts
2 tsp pine nuts

Remove excess fat from the ribs and cut into pieces, 6-8 cm in length. Pour the wine, soy sauce and sesame oil into a large shallow dish and add the shallot, spring onion, ginger, garlic, sesame seeds, sugar and pepper. Mix thoroughly until the sugar has dissolved, then add the ribs and stir to coat evenly. Set aside in the refrigerator for 1½ hours, turning the ribs occasionally.

Heat the oil in a large pan and sauté the onion for 2-3 minutes, then add the ribs and tomato and continue to cook over a moderately-hot heat, stirring frequently, until the ribs are well browned. Add 50 ml of the marinade and just sufficient water to cover the ribs and bring to the boil.

Lower heat, cover pan and simmer for approximately 1 hour, until the meat is tender, then uncover and bring back to the boil. Add water chestnuts, adjust seasonings to taste, and stir well. Cook over a high heat for 5 minutes to reduce the sauce, then transfer to a serving dish and garnish with pine nuts.

Vegetables

HEUNG SUI SHEUNG CHOI (braised vegetables); *recipe page 120*

HUNG SIU SHEUNG CHOI (braised vegetables)   *Hong Kong*

6 dried Chinese mushrooms
75 g dried wood ear mushroom
150 g eggplant
150 g white cabbage
150 g broccoli
2 carrots
1 green pepper
125 g can bamboo shoots, drained

75 ml vegetable oil
100 g bean curd, thinly sliced.
1 tsp finely chopped garlic
1 tsp finely chopped ginger
1 tsp finely chopped red chilli
1 tsp sugar
1 Tbsp light soy sauce
1 Tbsp oyster sauce

Soak the mushrooms in 400 ml warm water for 30 minutes, then discard the hard stems and halve the caps. Soak the wood ear mushrooms for 30 minutes, then slice thinly. Retain the water.

Prepare the vegetables and cut into bite-size pieces.

Heat half the oil in a wok and fry the bean curd until golden, then remove and drain. Add the vegetables to the wok and stir-fry for 1 minute, then remove and drain.

Heat a large clay pot over a fairly high heat, then add remaining oil. Allow to become very hot, then add the garlic and ginger and stir for 1 minute. Add the chilli, sugar, soy sauce, oyster sauce and reserved water and bring to the boil.

Add the vegetables, cover the pot and cook for 4-5 minutes, then add the bean curd, adjust seasonings to taste and cook for a further 2-3 minutes.

PINAKBET (vegetable casserole)   *Philippines*

1 Tbsp vegetable oil
125 g shallots, sliced
1 Tbsp crushed garlic
2 tsp finely chopped ginger
200 g pork crackling, diced
300 g small tomatoes, quartered

75 g anchovy paste
250 g eggplant, finely sliced
100 g okra
125 g bitter melons, quartered
salt to taste
freshly ground black pepper

Heat the oil in a casserole and add the shallot, garlic, ginger, pork crackling and tomato. Sauté until the oil has completely reduced, then add the anchovy sauce and bring to the boil.

Lower heat and allow to simmer until the sauce is thick, then add the eggplant, okra and bittermelon and adjust seasonings to taste. Cover the casserole and cook for a further 5 minutes, then serve immediately.

SAYUR GORENG (sautéed vegetables) — *Malaysia*

3 shallots, finely chopped
1 Tbsp finely chopped ginger
2 tsp finely chopped garlic
3 Tbsp peanut oil
8 cauliflower florets
4 carrots, sliced
1 green pepper, seeded and chopped
75 g green beans

12 baby corns
4 spring onions, chopped
3 Tbsp tomato sauce
2 Tbsp chilli sauce
1 Tbsp light soy sauce
0.5 tsp freshly ground black pepper
2 tsp sesame oil

Pound together the shallot, ginger and garlic with 1 Tbsp peanut oil to produce a smooth paste.

Heat the remaining oil in a wok and sauté the paste for 3-4 minutes, then add the cauliflower, carrot, green pepper, beans and corn and stir over a moderate heat until the vegetables are cooked but still crispy.

Add the tomato sauce, chilli sauce, soy sauce and 3 Tbsp water and bring to the boil, then add the spring onion and season with black pepper.

Cook for a further 2 minutes, stirring frequently, then transfer to a serving dish. Finally, heat the sesame oil and sprinkle over the vegetables.

TUMIS BAYEM (stir-fried spinach)   *Indonesia*

500 g spinach
1.5 Tbsp vegetable oil
2 shallots, finely chopped
3 fresh red chillies, finely chopped
2 tsp finely chopped ginger
1 tsp minced garlic
1 small tomato, finely chopped
2 curry leaves
1 tsp sugar
150 ml chicken stock
salt to taste
freshly ground black pepper
1 Tbsp crispy fried onion

Discard the stalks from the spinach and wash the leaves thoroughly under cold running water, then pat dry and chop into large bite-size pieces.

Heat the oil in a wok and stir-fry the shallot, ginger and garlic for 2-3 minutes, then add the chilli, tomato, curry leaves, sugar, soy sauce, pepper and stock and bring to the boil.

Stir well and cook for 1 minute, then add the spinach, bring back to the boil and continue to cook over a moderate heat for a further 2-3 minutes.

Discard the curry leaves, then transfer to a serving dish and top with crispy fried onion.

PAAD NAAM MUN HOY (broccoli in oyster sauce)   *Thailand*

350 g broccoli florets
1 Tbsp peanut oil
1 Tbsp finely chopped shallot
1 tsp minced garlic
3 Tbsp oyster sauce

1 Tbsp light soy sauce
1 tsp dark soy sauce
100 ml chicken stock
freshly ground black pepper
2 tsp finely chopped basil

Place the broccoli in a steamer and cook until tender but still crispy.

Heat the oil in a pan and sauté the shallot and garlic for 2 minutes, then add the oyster sauce, soy sauce and stock and bring to the boil. Add the broccoli and season with black pepper.

Cook for 2-3 minutes, stirring frequently, then transfer to a serving dish and garnish with finely chopped basil

GAN BIAN DAU (fried beans) — *Singapore*

450 g string beans
125 g fresh shrimps
oil for deep frying
75 g minced pork
2 tsp finely chopped ginger
75 g pickled vegetables, chopped
1 tsp minced garlic
2 tsp sugar
0.5 tsp freshly ground black pepper
1 Tbsp light soy sauce
75 ml chicken stock
2 tsp rice vinegar

Top and tail the beans and cut into 5 cm lengths. Shell and de-vein the shrimps and chop finely.

Heat the oil in a wok until it starts to smoke and fry the beans for 2-3 minutes, then remove with a slotted spoon and drain on kitchen paper. Pour away the oil and wipe the wok with a dry cloth. Replace the beans and stir over a high heat until they start to blacken, then remove and set aside.

Add 2 Tbsp oil to the wok and re-heat, then add the shrimp, pork, ginger, pickle and garlic and stir-fry for 2-3 minutes. Add the sugar, pepper, soy sauce and stock and bring to the boil, then replace the beans.

Retain over a high heat, stirring frequently, until the liquid has evaporated, then stir in the vinegar and cook for a further 30 seconds.

KARI BONCHI (curried beans) — *Sri Lanka*

200 g green beans
1 onion, finely chopped
1 tsp finely chopped garlic
4 curry leaves
2 fresh green chillies, finely sliced

0.5 tsp chilli powder
0.5 tsp ground coriander
0.5 tsp ground cumin
0.25 tsp ground turmeric
75 ml thick coconut milk

Trim the beans, wash and dry thoroughly and cut into 3 cm lengths.

Heat the oil and fry the onion and curry leaves for 4-5 minutes, then add the beans, fresh chilli, chilli powder, coriander, cumin and turmeric and continue to cook for a further 3 minutes, stirring frequently.

Add the coconut milk and cook until the beans are soft, then transfer to a dish and garnish with crispy fried shallot.

GAN LAN CAI MA TI (cabbage & water chestnuts) *China*

450 g Chinese cabbage
75 g straw mushrooms
125 g water chestnuts, thinly sliced
75 ml vegetable oil
400 ml chicken stock
1 tsp sugar
salt and freshly ground pepper

2 tsp finely chopped ginger
1 tsp minced garlic
2 Tbsp Chinese wine
2 Tbsp oyster sauce
2 tsp cornflour
1 Tbsp finely chopped spring onion

Discard stem and outside leaves and cut cabbage into serving-size pieces, then blanch in boiling water for 1 minute. Blanch the mushrooms for 1 minute.

Heat 3 Tbsp oil in a wok and stir-fry the cabbage and mushrooms for 1 minute, then remove and drain on kitchen paper. Add the chestnuts and stir-fry until golden, then remove and drain. Discard the oil.

Add 300 ml of stock to the wok and bring to the boil, then replace vegetables, add the sugar and season to taste with salt and pepper. Reduce the heat, cover the wok and allow to simmer for 5-7 minutes, then remove and drain. Discard the liquid.

Add remaining oil to the wok and stir-fry the ginger and garlic for 3 minutes, then add the wine, oyster sauce and remaining stock. Bring to the boil, replace the vegetables and stir for 2 minutes.

Finally, mix the cornflour with a little water and stir into the sauce to thicken, then transfer to serving dish and garnish with finely chopped spring onion.

DAHI ALOO (potatoes in yoghurt); TIL MOONGFALI ALOO (sesame potatoes)

DAHI ALOO (potatoes in yoghurt) *India*

500 g potatoes
3 Tbsp ghee
1 tsp cumin seeds
0.5 tsp mustard seeds
6 curry leaves
1 onion, finely chopped
6 green chillies, finely chopped
1 Tbsp finely chopped ginger

1 Tbsp garlic paste
1 tsp ground turmeric
150 ml natural yoghurt
2 dried red chillies, crushed
freshly ground black pepper
salt to taste
freshly chopped coriander leaves

Peel the potatoes and boil in lightly salted water, then drain and cut into cubes.

Heat the ghee in a pan, add cumin seeds, mustard seeds and curry leaves and cook until the seeds start to crackle, then add the onion, green chilli and ginger.

Cook until the onion becomes translucent, then add the garlic paste and turmeric and sauté for 5-6 minutes.

Whisk the yoghurt, add to the pan and bring to the boil, then add the potatoes, lower heat and allow to simmer for 2 minutes. Season with the crushed red chilli, salt and pepper and stir well, then transfer to a serving dish and garnish with freshly chopped coriander.

TIL MOONGFALI ALOO (sesame potatoes) *India*

500 g small new potatoes
3 Tbsp ghee
1 tsp cumin seeds
4 green chillies, finely chopped
1 Tbsp finely chopped ginger
1 Tbsp garlic paste
1 Tbsp white sesame seeds

2 Tbsp finely chopped peanuts
1 tsp roasted ground cumin
1 tsp red chilli powder
1.5 Tbsp freshly grated coconut
1 tsp garam masala
salt to taste
freshly chopped coriander leaves

Parboil the potatoes, then drain and set aside to cool.

Heat the ghee in a pan, add the cumin seeds, green chilli and ginger and cook until the seeds start to crackle, then add the garlic paste and sauté for 3 minutes.

Add the potatoes, sesame seeds, ground cumin, chilli powder, coconut, garam masala and salt and cook for a further 5-6 minutes, stirring frequently, then transfer to a serving dish and garnish with freshly chopped coriander.

ALA BUDUN (fried potato and onion) — *Sri Lanka*

450 g potatoes
1 tsp curry powder
0.25 tsp ground turmeric
0.25 tsp paprika
0.5 tsp salt
75 ml vegetable oil

2 large brown onions, sliced
4 curry leaves
0.5 tsp ground mustard seeds
20 mm cinnanmon stick
1 tsp fresh lime juice

Boil the potatoes, then drain and cut into bite-size chunks. Season with curry powder, turmeric, paprika and salt and set aside to cool.

Heat the oil in a large frying pan and add the onion, curry leaves, mustard and cinnamon stick. Stir fry until the onion are golden, then add the potato and cook for a further 2-3 minutes.

Remove the curry leaves and cinnamon stick, then transfer to a serving dish and sprinkle the lime juice on top.

BRINJAL MOJU (spiced eggplant) — *Sri Lanka*

400 g eggplant
0.5 tsp salt
0.5 tsp freshly ground black pepper
100 ml vegetable oil
1 green capsicum, thinly sliced
4 shallots, thinly sliced

1 Tbsp finely chopped ginger
1 tsp finely chopped garlic
1 tsp ground mustard seeds
0.5 tsp ground turmeric
50 ml vinegar
1 tsp sugar

Wash the eggplant under cold running water, then pat dry and cut into bite-size pieces. Season with salt and pepper and set aside for 20 minutes.

Heat the oil in a large frying pan and cook the eggplant for 4 minutes, stirring frequently, then remove and drain on kitchen paper. Add the green pepper and shallot to the pan and stir-fry for 3 minutes, then remove and drain.

Pour away most of the oil, then re-heat the pan, add the ginger and garlic and stir-fry for 3 minutes. Add the turmeric and vinegar and cook for 3 minutes, stirring frequently, then replace the eggplant, pepper and shallot and continue to cook for a further 5 minutes. Finally, adjust seasonings to taste, stir in the sugar and transfer to a serving dish.

ALA BUDUN (fried potato & onion); BRINJAL MOJU (spiced eggplant); KARI LEK (curried leeks)

KARI LEK (curried leeks)	*Sri Lanka*

400 g leeks
1 onion, finely sliced
2 green chillies, finely sliced
0.25 tsp ground turmeric
0.25 tsp salt

3 curry leaves
175 ml thin coconut milk
125 ml thick coconut milk
0.5 tsp curry powder

Wash the leeks under cold running water, then pat dry and cut into bite-size pieces. Place the leek, onion and chilli in a pan, add the turmeric, salt, curry leaves and thin coconut milk and bring to the boil.

Cook slowly until the liquid has almost evaporated, then add the thick coconut milk and bring back to the boil. Stir well and cook for a further minute, then remove curry leaves, transfer to a serving dish and sprinkle with curry powder.

YU XIANG QIE ZI (eggplant in hot garlic sauce)   *Taiwan*

350 g eggplants
3 Tbsp peanut oil
2 spring onions, finely chopped
3 fresh red chillies, finely chopped
1 Tbsp finely chopped ginger
1 Tbsp crushed garlic
75 g minced beef
2 tsp sugar
1 Tbsp Chinese wine
1 Tbsp soy sauce
100 ml chicken stock
2 tsp vinegar
1 tsp sesame oil

Wash and prepare the eggplants and cut into finger-size pieces. Heat the oil in a wok and fry the eggplant for 2 minutes, then remove and squeeze out excess oil.

Pour away most of the oil and re-heat the wok, then add the spring onion, chilli, ginger and garlic and stir-fry for 2 minutes. Add the beef and cook for a further 2 minutes, then add the sugar, wine, soy sauce and stock and bring to the boil.

Lower heat to moderate, then replace the eggplant, adjust seasonings to taste and continue to cook, stirring occasionally, until the liquid has reduced by two-thirds. Finally, stir in the vinegar and sesame oil and transfer to a serving dish.

YAKI NASU (grilled eggplant)   *Japan*

300 g small eggplants
0.5 tsp salt
0.25 tsp freshly ground white pepper
75 ml vegetable oil
2 tsp bonito flakes

Dip:
1.5 Tbsp finely shredded ginger
100 ml sweet soy sauce
1.5 Tbsp rice wine

Wash the eggplants and dry thoroughly, then halve lengthways. Score the flesh with a sharp knife and season with salt and pepper, then set aside for 30 minutes.

Brush eggplants with a little oil and cook under a hot grill, basting occasionally, until tender, approximately 20 minutes. Slice, arrange on a platter and sprinkle with bonito flakes.

Combine the ginger, soy sauce and wine and serve as a side dip.

BAGHARE BAINGAN (spicy and sour eggplant) — *Pakistan*

500 g small eggplants
75 g sesame seeds
75 g grated coconut
75 g ground peanuts
75 ml vegetable oil
1 Tbsp cumin seeds
1 tsp mustard seeds
0.5 tsp fenugreek seeds
8 curry leaves

1 Tbsp finely chopped ginger
2 tsp finely chopped garlic
1 Tbsp chilli powder
1 tsp ground turmeric
75 ml tamarind water
1 tsp ground coriander
1 tsp sugar
salt to taste
fresh coriander leaves

Wash and trim the eggplants and halve lengthways. Heat half the oil in a pan and fry the eggplants for 3 minutes, then remove and drain on kitchen paper.

Dry roast the sesame seeds, coconut and peanuts for 2 minutes, then pound with 2 tsp oil to produce a thick spice paste.

Heat the remaining oil in a clean pan and add the seeds and curry leaves. When the seeds start to crackle add the ginger and garlic and sauté for 3-4 minutes, then add the spice paste, chilli and turmeric.

Add the tamarind water and 75 ml of water and bring to the boil, then add the coriander, sugar and salt and allow to simmer for 3-4 minutes.

Replace the eggplants, stir to coat evenly with sauce and simmer for a further 2-3 minutes, then transfer to a serving dish and garnish with coriander leaves.

PANEER MUTTAR (feta cheese and pea curry) *India*

350 g feta cheese	*1 Tbsp finely chopped ginger*
200 g fresh green peas	*2 tsp finely chopped green chilli*
50 g ghee	*1 tsp red chilli powder*
5 green cardamom seeds	*0.5 tsp ground turmeric*
1 black cardamom seed	*1 Tbsp garlic paste*
5 cloves	*1 Tbsp ginger paste*
8 cm cinnamon stick	*4 tomatoes, skinned and chopped*
1 bay leaf	*salt to taste*
pinch of mace	*2 tsp garam masala*
2 onions, finely chopped	*1 Tbsp freshly chopped coriander*

Cut the cheese into small cubes and blanch the peas in boiling water.

Heat the ghee in a large pan and add the cardamoms, cloves, cinnamon stick and mace. Sauté over a moderate heat until the seeds start to crackle, then add the onion, ginger and green chilli. Cook until the onion is golden, then add the chilli powder and turmeric and stir well.

Dissolve the ginger and garlic pastes in a little cold water and add to the pan. Stir for 30 seconds, then add the tomato and salt to taste. Cook for 2 minutes, stirring continuously, then add 300 ml of water and bring to the boil.

Lower heat slightly, then add the feta cheese and peas and cook for 4-5 minutes, stirring occasionally. Finally, remove the cinnamon stick, add the garam masala and chopped coriander and stir for 30 seconds, then transfer to a serving dish.

RANG DONG GU (stuffed mushrooms) *Singapore*

12 dried Chinese mushrooms
200 g fresh shrimps
1 tsp salt
0.5 tsp freshly ground white pepper
2 tsp Chinese wine
1 tsp sesame oil
1 tsp cornflour
2 Tbsp finely chopped Yunan ham
freshly chopped coriander

Soak the mushrooms in warm water for 20 minutes, then pat dry and remove the hard stems. Shell and de-vein the shrimps and chop finely, then pound with the salt, pepper, wine, sesame oil and cornflour to produce a smooth paste.

Spread the paste on the underside of the mushrooms, then sprinkle with chopped ham and place in a steamer. Cook for 12-15 minutes, then transfer to a serving dish and garnish with freshly chopped coriander.

MATSUTAKE TSUTSUMI YAKI (grilled mushrooms) *Japan*

12 large dried black mushrooms
1 Tbsp light soy sauce
0.5 tsp freshly ground white pepper
75 ml rice wine

3 Tbsp sweet soy sauce
2 tsp fresh lemon juice
2 tsp sugar
2 tsp cornflour

Soak the mushrooms in warm water for 20 minutes, then pat dry and remove and discard the hard stems. Retain 75 ml of the water. Sprinkle the mushrooms with light soy sauce and pepper, then wrap in kitchen foil and cook under a hot grill for 10-12 minutes. Remove wrapping and arrange on a serving platter.

Meanwhile combine the reserved water, wine, soy sauce and lemon juice and bring to the boil. Add the sugar and stir for 2-3 minutes.

Mix the cornflour with a small quantity of cold water and stir into the sauce to thicken slightly, then spoon over the mushrooms and serve immediately.

DONG KU DAU FOO (bean curd with mushrooms) *Hong Kong*

6 dried Chinese mushrooms
300 g fresh bean curd
250 ml vegetable oil
2 shallots, finely chopped
1 Tbsp finely chopped ginger
1 tsp minced garlic

1 tsp sugar
0.5 tsp freshly ground white pepper
1 Tbsp Chinese wine
1 Tbsp light soy sauce
125 ml chicken stock
2 tsp cornflour

Soak the mushrooms in warm water for 20 minutes, then discard the hard stems and cut the caps in half. Soak the bean curd in cold water for 3 minutes, then drain and cut into bite-size pieces.

Heat the oil in a wok until it starts to smoke, then add the beancurd and fry until golden. Remove with a slotted spoon and drain on kitchen paper. Pour away all but 2 Tbsp oil and re-heat the wok, then add the shallot, ginger and garlic and stir-fry for 2 minutes.

Add the mushrooms and continue to stir for a further 2 minutes, then add the sugar, pepper, wine, soy sauce and stock and bring to the boil. Lower heat and replace the bean curd, then allow to simmer for 3 minutes.

Finally, mix the cornflour with a small quantity of cold water and stir into the sauce to thicken slightly, then transfer to a warm dish and serve immediately.

132

MA PO DOU FU (chilli bean curd) *Taiwan*

300 g fresh beancurd
2 Tbsp peanut oil
100 g minced pork
2 shallots, finely chopped
6 fresh red chillies, finely sliced
1 Tbsp finely chopped ginger,
4 cloves garlic, finely chopped

2 tsp hot bean paste
1 Tbsp light soy sauce
2 tsp dark soy sauce
1 Tbsp Chinese wine
175 ml chicken stock
freshly ground black pepper
1 Tbsp finely chopped spring onion

Soak the bean curd in cold water for 3 minutes, then drain and cut into chunks.

Heat the oil in a wok and stir-fry the pork for 3-4 minutes, then remove with a slotted spoon and drain on kitchen paper. Re-heat the oil, add the shallot, chilli, ginger and garlic and stir-fry for 3 minutes.

Replace the pork, add the bean paste, soy sauce, wine and stock and bring to the boil, then lower heat, add the bean curd and season to taste with black pepper.

Continue to cook, stirring frequently, for a further 3-4 minutes, then transfer to a serving dish and garnish with finely chopped spring onion.

Rice & Noodles

CHAU FAN (fried rice), *recipe page 136*

CHAU FAN (special fried rice) — Hong Kong

800 g long grain rice
125 g fresh baby shrimps
100 ml vegetable oil
2 shallots, finely chopped
2 tsp finely chopped ginger
1 tsp finely chopped garlic
1 Tbsp finely chopped red pepper
1 Tbsp finely chopped spring onion

100 g barbecued pork, shredded
75 ml chicken stock
1 Tbsp light soy sauce
salt to taste
freshly ground black pepper
2 eggs, lightly beaten
2 Tbsp crispy-fried onion

Boil the rice until tender, then set aside until cold. Shell and de-vein the shrimps.

Heat half the oil in a wok, add the shallot, ginger, garlic and red pepper and stir-fry for 2-3 minutes, then add the shrimps and spring onion. Continue to stir for a further minute, then remove mixture and drain on kitchen paper.

Pour the remaining oil into the wok and reheat, then add the rice and stir until the rice is warmed through. Replace the shrimp mixture, add the pork and stock and season with soy sauce, salt and pepper. Mix well.

Finally, add the egg and stir until the egg starts to set, then transfer to a serving dish and garnish with crispy fried onion.

KHAO PAAD SUPPAROD (pineapple rice) — Thailand

500 g long grain rice
1 large pineapple
100 g fresh shrimps
75 ml vegetable oil
1 shallot, finely chopped
2 fresh red chillies, finely sliced

1 tsp grated ginger
1 tsp minced garlic
125 g Chinese sausage, chopped
1 Tbsp light soy sauce
2 tsp fish sauce
freshly ground black pepper

Boil the rice until tender and fluffy, then set aside to cool. Halve the pineapple lengthways and carefully remove the flesh. Remove the hard core and stringy edges and cut the flesh into small dice. Clean the shells and set aside in a warm oven. Shell and de-vein the shrimps and chop into small pieces.

Heat the oil in a large wok, add the shallot, chilli, ginger and garlic and stir-fry for 2-3 minutes, then add the shrimp and sausage and season with soy sauce, fish sauce and pepper. Cook for a further minute, then add the rice and half the diced pineapple and stir until the rice is warmed through.

To serve, spoon the rice into the pineapple shells and garnish with remaining diced pineapple.

136

NASI GORENG (spicy fried rice) *Indonesia*

450 g long grain rice	3 Tbsp peanut oil
125 g fresh shrimps	125 g white chicken meat, diced
2 shallots, finely chopped	1 Tbsp light soy sauce
4 fresh red chillies, finely sliced	freshly ground white pepper
1 tsp chopped garlic	2 eggs, lightly beaten
2 tsp crumbled shrimp paste	2 tsp finely chopped spring onion

Soak the rice in cold water for 30 minutes, then rinse under running water and drain in a colander. Steam until tender and fluffy, then set aside.

Shell and de-vein the shrimps and halve, lengthways. Pound the shallot, chilli, garlic and shrimp paste with 2 tsp oil to produce a smooth paste.

Heat the remaining oil in a pan and stir-fry the spice paste for 5 minutes, then add the shrimps, chicken, soy sauce and pepper. Cook over a moderate heat for 3-4 minutes, then add the rice and stir well until the rice is hot.

Finally, increase the heat, add the egg, adjust seasonings to taste and stir until the egg begins to set, then transfer to a serving dish and garnish with finely chopped spring onion.

BRINGE (coconut rice)   *Philippines*

300 g long grain rice
50 ml vegetable oil
1 onion, finely chopped
2 tsp finely chopped ginger
2 tsp finely chopped garlic
150 white chicken meat, diced
150 g lean pork, diced
1 Tbsp fish sauce
75 ml chicken stock
300 ml thick coconut milk
75 g cooked peas
banana leaves
fresh red chillies, sliced

Soak the rice in cold water for 30 minutes, then drain in a colander.

Heat the oil in a pan, add the onion, ginger and garlic and sauté until the onion is translucent, then add the rice, chicken, pork, fish sauce and stock. Bring to the boil and cook over a moderate heat, stirring frequently, for 5 minutes, then pour in the coconut milk, adjust seasonings to taste and bring back to the boil.

Lower heat and allow to simmer until most of the liquid has evaporated, then stir in the peas. Cover the rice with banana leaves, press down slightly and cook for a further 4-5 minutes, until the rice is tender, then transfer to a platter covered with banana leaves and garnish with fresh red chillies.

KAHU BUTH (yellow rice)   *Sri Lanka*

450 Basmati rice
2 Tbsp ghee
1 small onion, thinly sliced
2 tsp finely chopped lemon grass
4 curry leaves
0.5 tsp ground cardamom

0.25 tsp ground cloves
0.5 tsp ground turmeric
8 cm cinnamon stick
salt to taste
freshly ground black pepper
650 ml thick coconut milk

Soak the rice for 2 hours, then rinse under cold water and drain.

Heat the ghee in a pan and fry the onion, lemon grass and curry leaves until the onion becomes translucent, then add the rice and stir for 2 minutes.

Add the cardamom, cloves, turmeric, cinnamon and coconut milk and bring to the boil. Stir over a fairly high heat for 3 minutes, then add seasonings, lower heat, cover the pan and cook until the liquid has been absorbed and the rice is light and fluffy.

MUTTAR PULAO (rice with peas) *India*

500 g Basmati rice
75 g ghee
5 green cardamoms
1 black cardamom
1 tsp cumin seeds
4 cloves
8 cm cinnamon stick

1 bay leaf
pinch of mace
1 tsp minced garlic
1 tsp finely grated ginger
150 g green peas
0.5 tsp salt
0.5 tsp freshly ground black pepper

Soak the rice in cold water for 30 minutes, then rinse under running water and drain in a colander.

Heat the ghee in a pan and add the cardamoms, cumin, cloves, cinnamon, bay leaf and mace. When the seeds starts to crackle add the garlic and ginger and stir over a moderate heat for 2 minutes, then add the peas and stir well.

Add the rice, season with salt and pepper and stir for 1 minute, then add 1 litre of boiling water, bring back to the boil and cook for 3-4 minutes. Cover the pan and reduce heat and cook until the water has evaporated and the rice is tender.

Remove the cinnamon stick and transfer the rice to a serving dish. Allow the steam to escape before fluffing the rice with a fork.

BIRYANI (rice with mutton)   *Pakistan*

500 g long grain rice   *2 onions, finely chopped*
2 candlenuts   *1 Tbsp finely chopped ginger*
8 cm cinnamon stick   *1 tsp minced garlic*
4 cloves   *salt to taste*
10 black peppercorns   *0.25 tsp saffron*
0.25 tsp ground turmeric   *6 fresh mint leaves*
0.25 ground anise   *6 fresh coriander leaves*
2 Tbsp ghee   *250 ml vegetable stock*

Parboil the rice, then drain and set aside. Pound the candlenuts, cinnamon, cloves, peppercorns, turmeric and anise with a little water to produce a paste.

Heat the ghee in a deep pan and sauté the onion, ginger and garlic for 3 minutes, then add the rice and continue to cook, stirring frequently, for 45 minutes. Add the spice paste and salt and stir to blend.

Place half the rice in a casserole, add the mutton, sprinkle with saffron and cover with remaining rice. Arrange the mint and coriander leaves on top, then pour in the stock and bring to the boil.

Cover with foil and place a tightly fitting lid on the casserole, then transfer to a pre-heated, moderately hot oven and cook until the liquid has been completely absorbed and the rice is tender, approximately 30 minutes.

LAKSA ASAM (sour soup noodles)   *Malaysia*

450 g rice vermicelli
800 g fish pieces, including heads
1 tsp salt
1 tsp freshly ground black pepper
2 onions, finely chopped
6 fresh red chillies, finely sliced
2 tsp finely chopped lemon grass

2 tsp crumbled shrimp paste
1 tsp ground turmeric
1.5 Tbsp sugar
50 ml tamarind water
50 g diced cucumber
50 g diced pineapple
fresh mint leaves

Place the noodles in a colander and scald with boiling water, then set aside.

Place the pieces of fish in a saucepan, add salt, pepper and 1.5 litres of water and bring to the boil, then lower heat, cover the pan and simmer for 1 hour. Allow the stock to cool, then strain through a fine sieve into a fresh saucepan and set aside. Discard the bones and skin and shred the meat.

Pound together the onion, chilli, lemon grass, garlic, shrimp paste and turmeric with 1 Tbsp of the fish stock to produce a smooth paste. Bring stock back to the boil, add the spice paste and the sugar and stir to dissolve, then add the fish and tamarind water. Cook over a moderate heat for 5 minutes.

Meanwhile, add the noodles to a pan of boiling water and cook for 3-4 minutes, then drain in a colander and transfer to a soup tureen. Pour boiling stock over the noodles, add the cucumber, pineapple and remaining onion and garnish with fresh mint leaves.

MI NAU CA VOI DUA (noodles in aromatic broth)   *Vietnam*

175 g egg noodles
1.5 Tbsp vegetable oil
4 spring onions, finely chopped
2 tsp finely chopped ginger
1 tsp finely chopped garlic
1 tsp finely chopped red chilli
1 Tbsp finely chopped coriander

1 tsp ground turmeric
150 g white fish fillet
1 litre clear fish stock
250 ml thin coconut milk
2 tsp fish sauce
0.5 tsp freshly ground black pepper
fresh basil leaves

Cook the noodles in boiling water for 1 minute, then drain in a colander.

Heat the oil in a pan, add the onion, ginger, garlic, chilli, coriander and turmeric and stir-fry for 1 minute, then add the fish and break into bite-size pieces. Add the stock and coconut milk and bring to a gentle boil, then add the noodles and season with fish sauce and pepper.

Cook until the noodles are tender, then transfer to a soup bowl and garnish with fresh basil leaves.

FUJIAN MIAN (spicy fried noodles) *Singapore*

500 g fresh egg noodles
200 g bean sprouts
200 g small fresh shrimps
150 g boiled squid
150 g roast pork
3 Tbsp peanut oil
2 shallots, finely chopped
6 fresh red chillies, finely chopped

2 tsp finely chopped ginger
1 tsp finely chopped garlic
100 ml chicken stock
2 spring onions, finely chopped
salt to taste
freshly ground black pepper
2 tsp dark soy sauce
2 eggs, lightly beaten

Bring a pan of water to a rapid boil and add the noodles. Remove pan from heat and let stand for 2 minutes, then drain noodles in a colander.

Wash and trim the bean sprouts. Shell and de-vein the shrimps and cut the squid and pork into fine shreds.

Heat half the oil in a wok and add the shallot, chilli, ginger and garlic. Stir-fry for 2 minutes, then add the shrimps, squid and pork. Stir for 2 minutes, then place a lid on the wok and cook for a further minute.

Remove lid, add the stock and bring to the boil, then add the bean sprouts, noodles and spring onion and season with salt and pepper. Cook for 1 minute, then add the remaining oil and soy sauce and stir well. Replace lid on the wok and cook for a further minute, then transfer to a serving dish.

Add the egg to the wok and stir over a moderate heat until the egg starts to set, then remove, cut into thin strips and arrange on top of the noodles.

MEEHUN GORENG (fried rice noodles) — *Indonesia*

250 g rice noodles	0.5 tsp ground coriander
125 g baby shrimps	0.5 tsp ground turmeric
125 g white chicken meat, diced	2 Tbsp tomato sauce
2 Tbsp vegetable oil	2 carrots, finely sliced
1 onion, finely chopped	1 Tbsp light soy sauce
2 tsp finely chopped ginger	2 tsp dark soy sauce
1 tsp finely chopped garlic	0.5 tsp freshly ground black pepper
1 tsp finely chopped lemon grass	2 tsp fresh lemon juice
1 tsp crumbled shrimp paste	3 spring onions, finely sliced

Cook the noodles in boiling water for 2 minutes, then pour into a colander and rinse under running water. Set aside to drain.

Shell and de-vein the shrimps and cut the chicken meat into fine slices.

Heat the oil in a wok, add the onion, ginger and garlic and sauté for 3 minutes, then add the lemon grass, shrimp paste, coriander, turmeric and tomato sauce. Stir to blend, then add the carrot, chicken and shrimps and cook for 2 minutes.

Add noodles, soy sauce and pepper and continue to cook, stirring frequently, for a further 3-4 minutes, then transfer to a serving dish, sprinkle with lemon juice and garnish with finely sliced spring onion.

Desserts

BUTT SZE PING GOR (toffee apples & bananas), recipe page 146

BA SI XIANG JIAO (toffee apples & bananas) *Singapore*

2 apples
4 bananas, ripe but firm
150 g plain flour
1 egg

peanut oil for deep frying
1 Tbsp sesame seeds
300 g sugar
sesame oil

Peel and core the apples and cut each into six slices. Peel and quarter the bananas, lengthways, then across and coat evenly with the batter..

Sift the flour and salt into a bowl. Beat the egg with 125 ml cold water, add to the flour and whisk to produce a smooth batter. Dip the pieces of fruit in the batter to coat evenly.

Heat the oil in a wok until it is very hot and deep-fry the pieces of fruit until golden, then remove with a slotted spoon, drain on kitchen paper and sprinkle with sesame seeds.

Meanwhile, place the sugar in a saucepan, add just sufficient water to cover and stir over a moderate heat until syrupy.

Coat the pieces of fruit with the hot caramel syrup and plunge into a bowl of iced water. Transfer to a plate lightly coated with sesame oil and serve while the sugary coating is hard.

KOLAK PISANG (stewed bananas in coconut milk) *Indonesia*

8 bananas (ripe but firm)
250 g soft brown sugar
100 g white sugar

3 pandan leaves
1 litre thick coconut milk
1.5 Tbsp cornflour

Cut the bananas into thick slices and place in a shallow saucepan. Add the lemon juice and just sufficient water to cover. Bring to the boil, then allow to simmer for 3-4 minutes until slightly softened. Drain on kitchen paper.

Add the sugar to the water in the pan, bring back to the boil and stir until the sugar is completely dissolved.

Add the coconut milk and again bring back to the boil. Remove a little liquid from the pan and mix with the cornflour, then return this to the pan and replace the banana slices.

Allow to simmer for a further 3 minutes, then transfer to a bowl and discard the pandan leaves. Serve immediately.

SHAI TUKRA (bread pudding)

India

8 slices white bread
75 g ghee
500 g granulated sugar
pinch of saffron
2 litres full fat milk

0.5 tsp ground cardamom
2 Tbsp almond slivers
2 Tbsp chopped pistachio nuts
edible silver leaf for garnish

Remove the crusts from the bread. Heat the ghee and fry the bread until golden, then quarter the slices diagonally.

Place the milk in a saucepan and bring to the boil, then lower heat slightly and leave to reduce for 30 minutes. Remove from heat and allow to cool, then stir in the cardamom.

Place the sugar in a saucepan, cover with water and bring to the boil. Lower heat and allow to simmer until the sugar has dissolved and the syrup is thick, then remove pan from the heat and stir in the saffron. Allow the syrup to cool, then add the bread and leave it to soak for 5 minutes.

Arrange the slices of bread on a large platter and cover with reduced milk. Sprinkle the almond slivers and pistachios on top and garnish with silver leaf.

BUBUR SANTEN (coconut pudding) — *Malaysia*

1.5 Tbsp gelatine powder
200 g soft brown sugar
400 ml thick coconut milk

2 tsp fresh lime juice
0.25 tsp vanilla essence
6 eggwhites

Warm 125 ml of water in a double boiler, sprinkle gelatine powder on top and stir until completely dissolved, then pour into a mixing bowl.

Add the sugar to 125 ml of boiling water and stir until completely dissolved, then allow to cool.

Add the syrup, coconut milk, lime juice and vanilla essence to the gelatine and place the bowl over a bed of shaved ice.

Beat the egg whites until stiff, then fold into the coconut syrup. Transfer to a dish, or individual moulds, and place in the refrigerator until set. Garnish with a little fruit.

GAJJAR HALWA (carrot dessert)   *India*

450 g carrots
600 ml fresh milk
200 g sugar
50 g ghee
2 Tbsp slivered almonds
2 Tbsp chopped pistachios
2 Tbsp raisins
0.25 tsp ground saffron

Scrape the carrots, then grate and place in a saucepan. Add 500 ml of the milk and 150 g of the sugar and bring to the boil. Lower heat and allow to simmer, stirring frequently, until the milk has evaporated.

Heat the remaining milk and sugar in a fresh saucepan and stir until the sugar has dissolved, then add to the carrot, together with the ghee. Stir well and cook over a moderate heat until the mixture starts to turn a golden brown, then add the almonds, pistachios and raisins.

Stir to blend thoroughly and cook for a further 2 minutes, then transfer to a serving dish and sprinkle the saffron on top.

WATALAPPAN (spiced coconut custard)   *Sri Lanka*

200 g palm sugar
250 ml thick coconut milk
5 fresh eggs, lightly beaten
few pinches ground cardamom
few pinches ground cinnamon
few pinches ground nutmeg
0.25 tsp rose essence
1 Tbsp cashew nuts

Place the palm sugar in a saucepan, add 150 ml cold water and bring to a slow boil. Stir until the sugar has dissolved then set aside to cool.

Break the eggs into a bowl and whisk lightly, then gradually add the coconut milk and syrup and continue to whisk until thoroughly blended.

Stir in the ground spices and the rose water and pour into a individual heatproof dishes and top with cashew nuts.

Place in a steamer and cook until set. Serve hot or cold.

GO LAKE DOU SAR (fried bean paste meringue) *Hong Kong*

5 egg whites
75 g custard powder
3 Tbsp castor sugar
0,5 tsp red food colouring

125 g sweet bean paste
1.5 Tbsp cornflour
oil for deep frying

Beat the egg whites in a bowl until fairly stiff, then blend in the custard powder and continue to beat until the mixture is very firm. In a shallow dish mix the sugar and food colouring and set to one side.

Mix the bean paste with a small quantity of cold water and shape into marble-size balls. Dust these with cornflour and dip into the egg mixture, allowing a considerable amount to stick (the finished meringue should be approximately 5 cm in diameter).

Heat the oil in a large wok until it starts to smoke, then lower heat slightly and deep-fry the meringues for approximately 2 minutes until golden.

Remove with a slotted spoon and drain off excess oil, then roll in the coloured sugar and serve immediately.

JO NAI WOO PAN (fried date pancakes) *Hong Kong*

150 g pitted dates, finely chopped
150 g granulated sugar
100 g sweet bean paste
oil for deep frying

6 cooked pancakes, kept warm
egg wash
3 Tbsp powdered sugar

Place the dates and sugar in a saucepan, add just sufficient water to cover and bring to the boil. Lower heat and simmer for 5 minutes, stirring frequently, then remove from heat and allow to cool.

Press the mixture through a fine sieve and combine with the bean paste. Heat 2 Tbsp of oil in a wok and stir-fry the mixture over a moderate heat for 5 minutes, then remove and drain on kitchen paper.

Spoon portions of the mixture on to the pancakes and fold the sides to secure, brush with egg wash.

Heat the remaining oil in a large wok until it starts to smoke, then lower heat slightly and deep-fry the pancakes, two at a time, until golden.

Remove with a slotted spoon and drain off excess oil, then dust with powdered sugar and serve immediately.

GUINATAAN (sago with fruit & yam) — *Philippines*

200 g sago pearls
250 g glutinous rice flour
1.5 litres thick coconut milk
225 g sweet potato, cubed
225 g purple yam, cubed

6 small bananas, sliced
250 g jackfruit, cut into small strips
200 g granulated sugar
200 ml coconut cream

Add the sago to a pan of boiling water and cook until it becomes transparent, then drain. Combine the rice flour with water and form into small balls.

Pour the coconut milk into a pan and bring to the boil. Add the sweet potato and yam and cook for 5 minutes, then add the banana, jackfruit, sago and rice balls and continue to cook until all the rice balls float to the surface.

Add the sugar and coconut cream and stir until the sugar has dissolved, then transfer to a serving bowl. Serve hot or cold.

KESARI KULFI (pistachio ice-cream) — *India*

5 litres full fat milk
2 large pinches of saffron
300 g sugar
0.5 tsp ground cardamom

2 Tbsp pistachio slivers
300 g cornflour
0.5 tsp food colouring
1 tsp rose syrup

Use 2 Tbsp milk to dissolve the saffron and pour the remainder into a large pan. Place the pan over a moderately-high heat and stir until the milk has reduced by half, then add the sugar and stir to dissolve.

Add the saffron, cardamom and pistachios and stir to blend thoroughly, then remove pan from the heat and set aside to cool. Pour the mixture into freezer trays and place in the freezer for at least 6 hours , stirring occasionally.

Bring 1.25 litres of water to the boil, then lower heat, add the cornflour and stir to dissolve. Add the food colouring and continue to stir until the liquid has reduced to a jelly-like consistency. Force through a sieve into a bowl of crushed ice, then arrange along the side of a serving dish.

Remove the ice-cream and cut into slices, then arrange on the plate and sprinkle with rose syrup.

SANGKAYA GAB KANOON (jackfruit custard)   *Thailand*

350 ml thick coconut milk
3 eggs
3 egg yolks
3 Tbsp castor sugar
2 tsp cornflour
150 g freshly chopped jackfruit

Pour the coconut milk into a pan and bring up to simmering point, then immediately remove pan from the heat and allow the milk to cool slightly.

Combine the eggs, egg yolks, sugar and cornflour and beat until creamy, then add to the coconut milk and stir to blend.

Replace pan over a low heat and stir well. Add the jack fruit and bring to simmering point, then immediately transfer to a heatproof bowl and cook in a steamer for 30 minutes.

Serve hot or cold

KAHA NIEW MAMUNG (sticky rice with mango)   *Thailand*

150 g glutinous rice
2 fresh mangoes
75 g sugar

200 ml thick coconut milk
1 tsp vanilla extract
pinch of salt

Soak the rice overnight, then cook in a steamer for 15-20 minutes. Allow to cool, then break up with a fork and transfer to a serving bowl.

Bring the coconut milk to a boil, add the sugar, salt and vanilla extract and stir until the sugar has dissolved, then remove from heat and allow to cool.

Remove flesh from the mangoes and cut into strips, then arrange on top of the rice. Pour in the sweetened coconut milk and chill before serving.

HALO HALO (salad of sweetened fruit and beans) *Philippines*

75 g red kidney beans,
75 g chick peas
sugar to taste
100 g cubed yam,
2 small bananas, sliced diagonally
100 g jackfruit, cut into strips

100 g coconut flesh, cut into strips
100 g bar red jelly
125 ml evaporated milk
shaved ice
6 scoops ice-cream

Boil the beans separately until tender, then add sugar to taste and let simmer for a further 15 minutes. Drain and set aside to cool.

Place the yam, banana, jackfruit and coconut in four separate pans of hot syrup and let simmer for 3 minutes, then remove and set aside to cool.

Soak the jelly in a pan of water for 10 minutes, then add sugar to taste and bring to the boil. Stir until the jelly has dissolved, then remove from heat, leave to set and cut into small cubes.

To serve, arrange layers of the beans, fruits and jelly in tall glasses, then pour in evaporated milk, add layers of shaved ice and top with scoops of ice-cream.

KESARI BUTH (semolina pudding) *Sri Lanka*

2 Tbsp ghee
125 g cashew nuts, coarsely chopped
125 g sultanas
200 g semolina

250 ml thin coconut milk
125 g date palm sugar
4 cardamom seeds, crushed
2 tsp rose water

Heat the ghee in a saucepan and stir-fry the cashew nuts until golden, then remove and drain on kitchen paper. Add the sultanas and fry for 2 minutes, then remove and drain.

Add the semolina to the pan and stir over a moderate heat for 3-4 minutes, then remove the pan from the heat.

In a fresh pan, heat the coconut milk and add the sugar. Stir until the sugar is completely dissolved, then pour over the semolina and bring to the boil.

Lower heat and cook until the liquid has been absorbed, then add the cashews, sultanas and cardamom and stir well.

Cook for a further minute, then transfer to a serving dish and sprinkle with rose water.

Glossary

AGAR AGAR
A natural tasting setting agent produced from various seaweeds. Has the advantage over commercial gelatine powders it stays firm in the hotter climates.

AJWAIN
A small seed with an unusual, anise-like flavour, used frequently in Indian cooking.

BAMBOO SHOOT
A cream coloured, conical-shaped vegetable frequently used in Asian cooking. When fresh must be peeled and boiled for some considerable time. Simpler to use the canned variety which unlike many vegetables retain their fresh flavour in the can.

BEAN CURD
Soy beans treated with an extract of rennet. Is highly nutritious and very popular particularly in China and Japan. Sold fresh in slabs and comes in a variety of flavours. Also know as tofu.

BEAN PASTE
Made with a base of soy beans and available in various flavours. Hot bean paste is flavoured with red chillies while the sweet variety uses sugar and seasonings.

BEAN SPROUTS
The sprouts of the green mung bean. Sold fresh in all Asian markets and many Western supermarkets. Served as a vegetable and used in many mixed stir-fries.

BLACHAN
A dried shrimp paste with an extremely pungent aroma used in the preparation of sambals. Is sold in small slabs and can be stored for lengthy periods in an air-tight container. Used frequently in Indonesian, Malaysian, Thai and Vietnamese cooking.

BLACK MUSHROOMS
Often referred to as Chinese mushrooms, they are sold dried and need soaking in warm water before using. The flavour is unique and there is no acceptable substitute.

CALAMANSI
A small and very juicy citrus fruit seldom found outside the Philippines. The flavour differs from both the lemon and lime but the latter may be used as a poor substitute.

CANDLENUT
An oily nut often used in the preparation of Indonesian and Malaysian curries. When unavailable, macadamia nuts make a good substitute.

CARDAMOM
A seed pod of the ginger family used whole or ground. It is very expensive which precludes its common use but it is an important ingredient in a number of recipes from Northern India and Pakistan.

COCONUT MILK
Obtained by grating the flesh of a mature coconut and squeezing with water. On average the flesh of one coconut added to 150 ml of warm water and squeezed through a fine muslin cloth will produce a thick milk. If a thinner milk is required further warm water should be added and again squeezed through the muslin. Note that the 'milky' liquid inside young green coconut makes a refreshing drink but is seldom used in cooking.

CORIANDER
Also known as Chinese parsley. The leaves, chopped or whole, are generally added towards the end of a cooking process or used as a garnish. The seeds, whole or ground are an essential ingredient of curry powders and pastes as well as being used in making cutneys. The root is also used, particularly in Thai cooking.

CUMIN
Another essential ingredient of curry powders, this small brown aromatic seed, generally ground before use has a slightly bitter taste

CURRY LEAVES
These small aromatic leaves, native to Southeast Asia, are best used fresh. When dried they lose much of their pungency, and as a result given quantities in any recipe should be increased by one third.

DIM SUM
A collective name for small, delicious Chinese snacks, fried and steamed, traditionally served from breakfast to lunch-time. The sweet varieties however are popular in the afternoon as well as being served as a conclusion to an evening meal. There are hundreds of varieties, many of which are time consuming to prepare so are more likely to be served in a restaurant than at home.

FENNEL
The leaves and seeds add a slightly aniseed like flavour and go particularly well with fish dishes.

FENUGREEK
The leaves, fresh and dried and the ground seeds provide another basic ingredient for curries. The flavour greatly enhances fish dishes but has a bitter taste and so should be used sparingly.

FIVE SPICE POWDER
A strong seasoning used a great deal in Chinese cooking and made from equal quantities of black peppercorns, fennel seeds, cinnamon bark, star anise and cloves.

GARAM MASALA

A vital ingredient in many Indian and Pakistani recipes. To make 250 g of **garam masala** place 50 g each of cloves, white and black cumin seeds, nutmeg and black peppercorns into a pan, add 25 g each of cinnamon bark and black cardamom seeds and place over a high heat. Cook for 10-12 minutes, stirring frequently, then pound in a mortar until fine and sift through a fine sieve before storing in an air-tight container.

GHEE

Pure butter fat with the milk solids removed. It may be heated to higher temperatures than butter and adds a distinctive flavour. If not available use clarified butter.

GINGER

Generally bought as a root stem and peeled, then sliced, grated or ground and with garlic and shallot (or onion) is the base for stir-fries, stews and curries. Occasionally pressed to produce a ginger juice, sometimes added at the end of the cooking as a condiment.

GINGKO NUTS

Used in Japanese cooking. Available in cans.

GLUTINOUS RICE

A variety of long-grain rice which becomes sticky and transparent when cooked.

HOI SIN SAUCE

A sweet and spicy sauce often served as a side dish with Chinese meat and poultry.

KAFFIR LIMES

Somewhat larger than the more familiar limes sold in Western markets, the fruit has a knobbly skin and a very sharp, aromatic flavour. The skin, pulp and leaves are all used frequently in Thai cooking.

LEMON GRASS

An aromatic grass with a small bulbous root, which when crushed gives a strong lemon flavour. It can often be found in powdered form and labelled **serai.**

ONION SEEDS

Occasionally used in Indian curries and generally sold in Asian markets as **kalongi**

OYSTER SAUCE

Made from oysters boiled in salted water, then pureed. It adds a delicious extra flavour to many Chinese meat and vegetable dishes.

PALM SUGAR

A hard brown sugar made from the juice of the coconut palm flower. Generally crushed or grated before use.

PANDAN LEAVES

Can be used whole in cooking and removed prior to serving or pounded with a little cold water and used as a paste. Often used as a natural green food colouring.

SAMBAL

A popular side dish throughout the region made from grinding together chillies, blachan (shrimp paste), and salt, then stored until required in an airtight container. Before using, mix a small amout with sugar and fresh lime juice. Quantities must depend on personal tastes but it is generally served as a very hot (as in spicy-hot) dip.

SESAME OIL

A strong oil with a slightly nutty flavour, made from roasted sesame seeds. Very small quanities will enhance the flavour when used in cooking or in side dips. It is never used as a cooking oil.

SHRIMP PASTE

(See **'BLACHAN',** also introduction, page 11)

SOY SAUCE

An absolute essential in every Asian kitchen. There are many types of soy sauce, the most commonly used one being light in both colour and flavour and adding a salty taste to dishes and dips. The dark soy sauce referred to in some of the proceeding recipes is used less frequently and more sparingly. A sweet variety is used in Japan and occasionally in South East Asia.

SZECHUAN PEPPERCORNS

Brown in colour the addition of these peppercorns adds a pleasant aroma and a mildly hot flavour.

TAMARIND WATER

Produced by soaking dried tamarind in warm water for 10 minutes, then straining through a fine sieve. It is frequently used in curries and adds a distinctive and very sour taste.   Only used in small quantities.

TURMERIC

Packaged already ground (although the root is also available in many Asian markets), this bright orange spice, a member of the ginger family is an essential ingredient in making curry powder.

WATER CHESTNUTS

Small bulbs with a tough brown skin and a white flesh, which when grated, or finely chopped, adds a crunchy texture to many poultry, meat and vegetable stir-fries. Easily obtained in cans and will keep for some time when the water is changed regularly.

WON TUN WRAPPERS

Squares of very thin dough, made with a high gluten flour and readily available fresh in specialist Chinese stores. Also sold frozen in many supermarkets. Used to encase various fillings for dim-sum and also in soups.

YAM

A root vegetable, native to Asia, with a mild, slightly sweet flavour. The outer bark is removed before cooking and it can then be roasted and served as a vegetable or mashed and used in desserts and cakes.